Forensic Accounting

Hashem Alshurafat

Forensic Accounting

Practice and Theory

Springer

Hashem Alshurafat
Department of Accounting, Business School
The Hashemite University
Zarqa, Jordan

ISBN 978-981-95-8612-7 ISBN 978-981-95-8613-4 (eBook)
https://doi.org/10.1007/978-981-95-8613-4

This Springer imprint is published by the registered company Springer Nature Singapore Pte Ltd.
The registered company address is: 152 Beach Road, #21-01/04 Gateway East, Singapore 189721, Singapore

Preface

Today's business environment is highly dynamic and complex. Therefore, there is a need for professionals who can master multidisciplinary skills and knowledge to bridge the gap between other professionals and solve vexing problems. Forensic accountants possess a range of skills and knowledge from fields such as law, business, accounting, and technology. This knowledge and these skills enable them to connect clients, judges, lawyers, and business leaders to solve a range of problems, including fraud cases, financial disputes, and legal matters.

This book aims to illustrate the role of forensic accountants in today's business environment and the services they provide. These services include roles in fraud investigation, litigation support, business valuation, and IT forensics. By highlighting these services and roles, this book enriches our understanding of the important roles forensic accounting practitioners play in today's business environment.

Zarqa, Jordan

Hashem Alshurafat

Competing Interests The author has no competing interests to declare that are relevant to the content of this manuscript.

Contents

1 Overview of the Forensic Accounting Profession 1
- 1.1 Introduction 1
- 1.2 Forensic Accounting Roles 2
- 1.3 The Importance of Forensic Accounting 2
- 1.4 The Strengths and Weaknesses of Forensic Accounting ... 4
- 1.5 Professional Opportunities for Forensic Accountants ... 4
- 1.6 Professional Certificates Available for Forensic Accountants 5
- 1.7 Concluding Remarks 6
- References 7

2 Forensic Accounting Ethics: Authoritative Guidance and Non-Authoritative Guidance 9
- 2.1 Introduction 9
- 2.2 Ethical Values of the Forensic Accounting Profession: Prior Studies Evidence 10
- 2.3 Ethical Code of Conduct for Forensic Accountants: From the Jordanian Perspective 11
  - 2.3.1 IESBA/International Code of Ethics, Adopted in Jordan via HCAP/JACPA 11
  - 2.3.2 Jordan Integrity & Anti-Corruption Law/Integrity & Anti-Corruption Commission (JIACC) 11
  - 2.3.3 Anti-Money-Laundering & Counter-Terrorist-Financing (AML/CFT) Law & AMLU (Financial Intelligence Unit) 13
  - 2.3.4 Companies Law (No. 22/1997) and Amendments (Including Law No. 19/2021 and Later Updates) 13
  - 2.3.5 Penal Code/Criminal Law (Fraud, Embezzlement, Falsification Offences) 14
  - 2.3.6 Central Bank of Jordan (CBJ) Rules & Banking Law/Sectoral Regulations 14
  - 2.3.7 Jordan Securities Commission (JSC Rules & Corporate Governance Code) 14

2.3.8 Regulatory/Professional Frameworks & Oversight Bodies . . . 15
2.3.9 International Conventions and Regional Instruments 15
2.3.10 Evidence, Criminal Procedure, and Court Practice Rules . . . 15
2.4 International Ethical Codes of Conducts 16
2.5 Conclusion 16
Appendix: Ethical Situations 19
References. 22

3 Forensic Accounting Role in Fraud Investigation, Prevention, and Mitigation 25
3.1 Introduction 25
3.2 What Is Fraud?. 25
3.3 Fraud Tree 26
3.3.1 Occupational Fraud 26
3.3.2 External Fraud 28
3.3.3 Individual Fraud. 33
3.4 Fraud Impact 34
3.5 Investigation Tools 35
3.5.1 Behavioral Indicators Approach to Investigate Fraud 36
3.5.2 Prevention and Mitigation Tools 38
3.6 Conclusion 40
References. 40

4 The Role of Forensic Accounting in Detecting and Deterring Organised Financial Crimes 43
4.1 Introduction 43
4.2 Money Laundering. 43
4.2.1 The Definition and Impact of Money Laundering. 43
4.2.2 Steps for Conducting Money Laundering 44
4.2.3 Scenarios and Cases for Money Laundering 45
4.2.4 The Role of Forensic Accountants in Detecting Money Laundering. 46
4.3 High-Profile Corporate Scandals 47
4.3.1 The Definition and Impact of High-Profile Corporate Scandals 47
4.3.2 Examples of High-Profile Corporate Scandals 47
4.3.3 Reasons Behind the High-Profile Corporate Scandals. 48
4.3.4 The Role of Forensic Accounting Practitioners in Detecting Identity Theft 48
4.4 Ponzi and Pyramid Schemes 49
4.4.1 The Definition and Impact of Ponzi and Pyramid Schemes. 49
4.4.2 How the Ponzi Scheme Works?. 49
4.4.3 How Pyramid Scheme Work? 49
4.5 Identity Theft 50
4.5.1 The Definition and Impact of Identity Fraud. 50

4.5.2 The Role of Forensic Accounting Practitioners in Detecting Identity Theft . . . 50
4.6 Conclusion . . . 50
References . . . 51

5 The Role of Forensic Accountants in Litigation Support . . . 55
5.1 Introduction . . . 55
5.2 The Role of Forensic Accountants Within the Courts . . . 56
5.2.1 Expert Witness . . . 56
5.2.2 Expert Consulting . . . 57
5.3 The Role of Forensic Accountants Outside the Courts (Financial Dispute Resolutions) . . . 57
5.3.1 Negotiation . . . 58
5.3.2 Mediation . . . 58
5.3.3 Arbitration . . . 59
5.3.4 Advantages and Disadvantages of Alternative Dispute Resolution . . . 59
5.4 Other Litigation Support Services . . . 59
5.5 Qualifications for an Expert Witness . . . 60
5.6 Ethics, Skills, and Knowledge Required for Forensic Accountants in Litigation Support . . . 61
5.7 Conclusion . . . 61
References . . . 63

6 The Role of Forensic Accounting in Business Valuation Services . . . 67
6.1 Introduction . . . 67
6.2 Business Valuation Services . . . 68
6.2.1 Long-Term Employee Incentive . . . 68
6.2.2 Death and Personal Injury . . . 68
6.2.3 Matrimonial Issues and Hidden Asset Investigations . . . 69
6.2.4 Superannuation Interests . . . 69
6.2.5 Insolvency and Bankruptcy . . . 69
6.2.6 Loss and Damage Claims . . . 69
6.2.7 Calculating Profits Lost . . . 70
6.2.8 Business Interruption . . . 70
6.2.9 Breaches of Contract Loss . . . 70
6.2.10 Minority Interests . . . 70
6.2.11 Insurance Claims . . . 70
6.2.12 Intellectual Property . . . 71
6.2.13 SWOT Analysis . . . 71
6.2.14 Merger and Acquisition . . . 71
6.2.15 Reconstruction Records . . . 71
6.2.16 Deliver Estimation of Value . . . 71
6.3 Conclusion . . . 72
References . . . 72

7 The Role of Forensic Accounting in Detecting and Preventing Digital and Online Crimes 77
7.1 Introduction 77
7.2 The Nature of Forensic Accountant Work in the Digital Environment 78
7.3 Skills and Knowledge for a Forensic Accountant in IT Forensics . . . 78
7.4 Computer Forensics Responsibilities 79
7.5 Qualifications 79
7.6 Digital Forensics Labs 80
7.7 Sub IT Forensic Services 81
7.8 E-Mail Investigation Cases 81
7.9 Investigation Tools 82
7.10 Forensics Software Tools 82
7.11 Scenarios for Forensic Accounting Investigation Within the IT Forensic Services 83
7.12 Conclusion 84
References 84

Index 87

About the Author

Hashem Alshurafat is an academic in the field of accounting, ranked among the top 2% of scientists worldwide in 2024 by the Stanford University ranking system. His scholarly contributions have been acknowledged through several prestigious awards, including the Best Reviewer Award from Emerald Publishing and the Best Paper Award from the AL-Hussain Fund. He currently serves as Associate Professor of Accounting at Hashemite University, where he also serves as Deputy Dean. Dr. Alshurafat earned his PhD in Accounting from the University of Southern Queensland in Australia, an experience that equipped him with a strong foundation in critical accounting theories and practices. Beyond his teaching responsibilities, he is actively engaged in the academic community as an editor and reviewer for numerous scholarly journals. He is a member of the editorial teams of *SAGE Open* and *Discover Sustainability*. He has served as a guest editor for special issues of the journals *Journal of Financial Reporting and Accounting*, *Discover Sustainability*, and *Sustainability*. Through these roles, he has played a key part in supporting and advancing high-quality academic research. Dr. Alshurafat has also contributed to the publication of five edited books with well-respected publishers, including Springer and Emerald. His research interests encompass forensic accounting, sustainability in business practices, the integration of technology in accounting, and accounting education. His work has been published in leading academic journals and presented at international conferences indexed in Scopus and Web of Science. Through his ongoing research, teaching, and service, he continues to advance the accounting discipline.

Chapter 1
Overview of the Forensic Accounting Profession

1.1 Introduction

In today's business environment, forensic accounting has gained significant importance due to the need to supervise complex financial transactions to prevent litigation and fraud risks [1]. Furthermore, forensic accountants have demonstrated high-level expertise in business valuation services and IT forensic solutions. Forensic accounting is a modern subspecialty within accounting. However, there is a notable difference between forensic accounting, auditing, and accounting itself [2].

Crain et al. [2] define forensic accounting as "Forensic accounting involves the application of special skills such as accounting, auditing procedures, finance, quantitative methods, research, and investigations. It also involves knowledge of certain areas of the law. This knowledge, combined with these skills enable forensic accountants to collect, analyze, and evaluate evidential matter and to interpret and communicate findings." Moreover, most forensic accounting studies propose three levels for defining forensic accounting. The first, the narrower definition, focuses solely on forensic accounting's investigative role and describes it as a tool for fraud detection and prevention. The second level, which encompasses a broad definition, primarily focuses on the forensic accounting services that professional bodies can provide in support of fraud and litigation. The third level, which is the more comprehensive definition, focuses on the four main services of forensic accounting (i.e., litigation support, business valuation, fraud investigation, and IT forensics) [3–7].

Forensic accounting emerged in the early twentieth century to provide expert testimony in legal proceedings and assess financial damages in civil lawsuits. The field expanded in the 1960s and 1970s due to rising white-collar crime, and it gained formal recognition with the establishment of the Association of Certified Fraud Examiners in 1988 [8]. The 1990s witnessed a significant rise in its use, spurred by high-profile financial scandals such as Enron, which increased demand for forensic accounting services in corporate investigations and litigation [9]. In the twenty-first

H. Alshurafat, *Forensic Accounting*, https://doi.org/10.1007/978-981-95-8613-4_1

century, forensic accounting has become vital for detecting and preventing fraud, supporting corporate governance. It has broadened to include digital forensics, anti-money laundering, and other financial crimes as its importance has grown alongside the rise in economic crime [10].

1.2 Forensic Accounting Roles

Generally, forensic accountants offer services in four primary categories. Firstly, forensic accountants provide litigation support services [11]. These services can be classified into two main areas: inside the court (expert witness and expert consulting) and outside the court (dispute resolution) [12]. Secondly, forensic accounting practitioners tend to engage in business valuation assignments [13]. Financial institutions rely on forensic experts to maintain credibility and trust. Furthermore, forensic accountants are hired to resolve disputes over insurance claim valuations. Thirdly, forensic accountants deliver essential services in fraud detection and prevention [14]. Finally, forensic accounting practitioners provide services to prevent and detect electronic financial crimes [15]. It is important to note that professionals in this field often specialise in one area. For instance, you may come across a forensic accountant who is an expert in business valuation but lacks expertise in fraud examination, or vice versa. Figure 1.1 displays the index of forensic accounting services.

1.3 The Importance of Forensic Accounting

Recently, the need for and importance of forensic accounting have increased due to several reasons. Many universities worldwide have integrated forensic accounting into their accounting curricula [17]. Furthermore, the big 4 audit firms have established forensic accounting teams to oversee adversarial and investigative assignments from their clients. Additionally, the number of firms dedicated to forensic accounting services is increasing. For instance, in the Australian context, more than 40 firms provide one or more of the forensic accounting services [18]. The following are the reasons why the forensic accounting profession has gained significance in recent decades.

1. An increase in fraud and corporate scandals worldwide.
2. The complexity of financial lawsuits.
3. An increase in corporate regulatory compliance.
4. Growth in litigation and disputes.
5. The sophistication of business transactions in the digital era.
6. An increase in digital financial crimes.
7. Increased demand for insurance valuation claims.

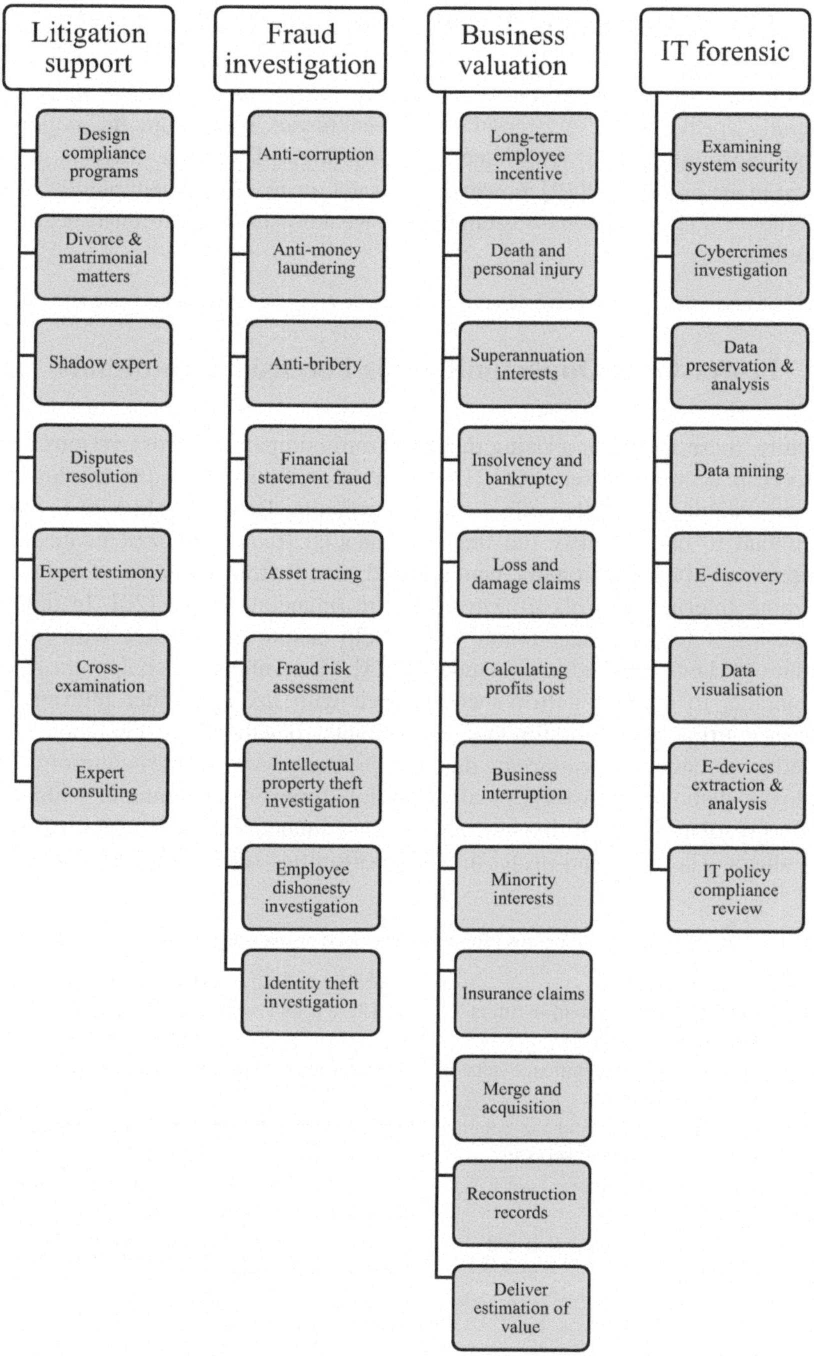

Fig. 1.1 Forensic accounting service index. Source: Adopted from Alshurafat [16]

1.4 The Strengths and Weaknesses of Forensic Accounting

As with any profession, forensic accounting has its strengths and weaknesses. Generally speaking, these strengths and weaknesses stem from the notion that forensic accounting is a new branch of accounting. Therefore, there is growing interest in the profession [19]; however, it has not received sufficient public recognition. Table 1.1 shows the main strengths and weaknesses of the forensic accounting profession.

1.5 Professional Opportunities for Forensic Accountants

Recently, there has been a rising demand from companies across various sectors for forensic accounting services [21]. Moreover, some firms tend to employ forensic accountants within their financial departments. Banks might hire a forensic accountant to help identify red flags of financial fraud, embezzlement, or asset misappropriation. Additionally, banks would benefit from a forensic accountant in designing internal controls to prevent future financial crimes [22]. In industrial companies, a forensic accountant would help ensure compliance with financial regulations, laws, and industry standards [23]. Governments also appoint forensic accountants to oversee a firm's compliance with tax and other relevant laws. Insurance firms may hire forensic accountants to validate or challenge claims related to revenue loss, economic damage, property loss, business interruption, or employee dishonesty. Attorneys also employ forensic accountants within their firms to resolve financial disputes and address financial fraud committed against individuals. The roles and professional opportunities for forensic accountants are

Table 1.1 Strengths and weaknesses of the forensic accounting profession

Strength	Weakness
(1) Forensic accounting education offers substantial benefits to students	(1) There is an absence of established professional standards and regulatory bodies
(2) The profession holds significant value in the business and legal fields	(2) Entry into the profession is not well-regulated
(3) There is a growing demand and notable need for forensic accounting services	(3) Educational programs in forensic accounting lack consistency in their content.
(4) It opens up new and diverse career opportunities	(4) There is a shortage of academic research and dedicated journals in the field
(5) It contributes to the prevention and detection of fraud	(5) The core purpose of forensic accounting is often misunderstood
	(6) There is a need for highly qualified professionals and educators
	(7) The profession lacks widespread public recognition and has a relatively low reputation

Source: Adopted from [20]

diverse and widespread. Table 1.2 illustrates the sectors in which a forensic accountant might work.

Within the sectors and industries mentioned above, a forensic accounting practitioner could be engaged to handle various assignments. As discussed earlier in this chapter, there are four main categories of forensic accounting services; the following are the primary professional opportunities for a forensic accountant.

Litigation support services:

Expert witness: A forensic accountant might be appointed by a court to provide technical and professional testimony to support the jury and the judge.

Consultant: A forensic accountant may be appointed by any party in the litigation process to offer technical and professional advice.

Mediator: A forensic accountant may be appointed by any party in a financial dispute to reconcile different viewpoints between disputing parties.

Arbitrator: A forensic accountant may be appointed by any party in a financial dispute to provide a judgment to settle the dispute between disputing parties.

Fraud investigation:

Fraud examiner: A forensic accountant may be appointed to assess fraud risk, prevent fraud, and investigate fraud cases within government agencies, private firms, or on an individual level.

Business Valuation:

Appraiser: A forensic accountant may be appointed to provide asset quantification and valuation services, as well as economic damage services.

IT forensics:

Computer forensic scientist: A forensic accountant may be appointed to organise and interpret digital evidence and provide reports to investigate financial electronic crimes.

1.6 Professional Certificates Available for Forensic Accountants

Numerous professional bodies and certifications are relevant to forensic accountants, each providing unique advantages based on an individual's background and specialisation. Leading organisations require strict ethical standards and continuous education to retain credentials.

The Certified Forensic Accountant (Cr.FA) is awarded by the American Board of Forensic Accounting (ABFA) and specialises in forensic accounting, litigation support, and investigative skills. The American Institute of Certified Public Accountants (AICPA) offers the Certified in Financial Forensics (CFF) and Accredited in Business Valuation (ABV) qualifications, both of which require exams and

Table 1.2 The role of forensic accountants across industry sectors: reasons for hiring

Firm sector	Reasons to hire a forensic accountant
Banking	To detect financial fraud, money laundering, and ensure regulatory compliance
Insurance	To investigate suspicious claims, assess claim validity, and prevent insurance fraud
Industrial firms	To uncover internal fraud, misappropriation of assets, and support litigation in contract disputes
Retail & consumer	To identify inventory theft, vendor fraud, and financial statement manipulation
Healthcare	To detect billing fraud, overcharges, and ensure compliance with healthcare regulations
Technology firms	To investigate intellectual property theft, cybercrime, and financial misconduct
Construction	To audit project costs, investigate contract fraud, and support claims in construction disputes
Energy & utilities	To assess regulatory compliance, uncover corruption, and investigate misreporting of environmental costs
Government	To detect misuse of public funds, corruption, and ensure transparency in financial reporting
Legal firms	To provide expert witness services and support complex financial litigation cases

professional experience. The American Society of Appraisers (ASA) offers designations such as Accredited Member (AM) and Accredited Senior Appraiser (ASA), which promote high ethical standards and continuous professional development. The Association of Certified Fraud Examiners (ACFE) grants the Certified Fraud Examiner (CFE) credential, focusing on fraud prevention and detection, and is open to accountants and professionals from other fields.

ISACA provides credentials essential for forensic accountants working with information systems, including Certified Information Systems Auditor (CISA), Certified in Risk and Information Systems Control (CRISC), and Certified Information Security Manager (CISM). The National Association of Certified Valuators and Analysts (NACVA) supports specialists in business valuation and litigation services by offering training and ongoing education, while requiring adherence to a code of ethics. Table 1.3 shows the professional certificates available for forensic accountants.

1.7 Concluding Remarks

In conclusion, today's complex and rapidly changing business environment requires forensic accountants to investigate and prevent fraud, simplify complex financial transactions, testify in court for financial lawsuits, resolve financial disputes, quantify economic damage, and detect electronic financial crimes. Forensic accountants

Table 1.3 The professional certificates available for forensic accountants

Certification	Issuing organization	Description	Website
Certified Forensic Accountant (Cr.FA)	American Board of Forensic Accounting (ABFA)	Focuses on forensic accounting, litigation support, and investigative skills	https://www.abfa.us
Certified Fraud Examiner (CFE)	Association of Certified Fraud Examiners (ACFE)	Specializes in fraud prevention, detection, and investigation	https://www.acfe.com
Certified in Financial Forensics (CFF)	American Institute of Certified Public Accountants (AICPA)	Credential for CPAs with forensic accounting experience	https://www.aicpa.org
Certified Forensic Auditor (CFA)	American Board of Forensic Auditors (ABFA)	Emphasizes auditing procedures and forensic examination	https://www.abfa.us
Certified Forensic Financial Analyst (CFFA)	National Association of Certified Valuators and Analysts (NACVA)	Focuses on financial litigation and forensic analysis	https://www.nacva.com
Certified Valuation Analyst (CVA)	National Association of Certified Valuators and Analysts (NACVA)	While primarily for valuation, includes forensic elements	https://www.nacva.com
Forensic Certified Public Accountant (FCPA)	Forensic CPA Society	Recognizes expertise in forensic accounting practices and litigation support	https://www.fcpas.org
Diploma in Forensic Accounting	Chartered Institute of Management Accountants (CIMA) (UK)	Offers training in financial crime and fraud risk management	https://www.cimaglobal.com

play different roles within organisations across the public and private sectors. Therefore, forensic accounting has received increasing attention. Moreover, many organisations offer credentials to new forensic accountants after a rigorous examination and experience validation process. This chapter focuses on the roles of forensic accounting, its strengths and weaknesses, certification, and professional opportunities in the field. This chapter aims to help students, academics, and regulators understand the essentials of forensic accounting.

References

1. Ozili, P.K., *Forensic accounting research around the world.* Journal of Financial Reporting and Accounting, 2025. **23**(1): p. 128–153.
2. Crain, M.A., et al., *Essentials of forensic accounting*. 2019: John Wiley & Sons.
3. Botes, V. and A. Saadeh, *Exploring evidence to develop a nomenclature for forensic accounting.* Pacific Accounting Review, 2018. **30** (2): p. 135–154.
4. Alkababji, M.W., et al., *Forensic Accounting Practices: Evaluating the Current Research*, in *Achieving Sustainable Business Through AI, Technology Education and Computer Science:*

Volume 3: Business Sustainability and Artificial Intelligence Applications. 2024, Springer. p. 767–777.
5. Guellim, N., et al., *Evaluating the perceived value of forensic accounting: a systematic review method.* Discover Sustainability, 2024. **5**(1): p. 351.
6. Ahmad, S., M.S. Ibrahim, and R.M. Abdou, *Understanding the Role of Forensic Accountants in Due Diligence Within Organizations and Its Impact on Organizational Learning.* Sustainable Data Management: Navigating Big Data, Communication Technology, and Business Digital Leadership. Volume 1, 2025: p. 3–10.
7. Ismail, S., R.M. Abdou, and M.S. Ibrahim, *Who is Better in Practicing Customer Due Diligence as an Anti-Money Laundering Tool for Financial Institutions: Can Internal Auditors Be Forensic Accountants? Evidence from MENA Region*, in *Sustainable Data Management: Navigating Big Data, Communication Technology, and Business Digital Leadership. Volume 1*. 2025, Springer. p. 11–23.
8. Rezaee, Z., D.L. Crumbley, and R.C. Elmore, *Forensic accounting education: A survey of academicians and practitioners.* Advances in Accounting Education Teaching and Curriculum Innovations, 2004. **6**: p. 193–231.
9. Curtis, G.E., *Legal and regulatory environments and ethics: Essential components of a fraud and forensic accounting curriculum.* Issues in Accounting Education, 2008. **23**(4): p. 535.
10. Curtis, G.E., *The model curriculum in fraud and forensic accounting and economic crime programs at Utica College.* Issues in Accounting Education, 2008. **23**(4): p. 581–592.
11. Al-Hazaima, H., O. Arabiat, and G. Maayah, *The double-edged sword of forensic accounting services: litigation risks in Jordan's industrial sector.* Journal of Financial Reporting and Accounting, 2023.
12. Abdul-Baki, Z., *The role of accounting in conflicts resolution: The case of PwC's forensic audit of the Nigerian National Petroleum Corporation.* Managerial Auditing Journal, 2019. **36** (2): p. 261–279.
13. DiGabriele, J.A. and P.L. Lohrey, *The valuation of economic damages: A case study for the forensic accountant.* Journal of Forensic and Investigative Accounting, 2016. **8**(2): p. 338–348.
14. Oyerogba, E.O., *Forensic auditing mechanism and fraud detection: the case of Nigerian public sector.* Journal of Accounting in Emerging Economies, 2021. **11**(5): p. 752–775.
15. Pearson, T.A. and T.W. Singleton, *Fraud and forensic accounting in the digital environment.* Issues in Accounting Education, 2008. **23**(4): p. 545.
16. Alshurafat, H., *New variables and measurements of forensic accounting: implications on financial reporting and auditing.* Discover Sustainability, 2024. **5**(1): p. 376.
17. Rezaee, Z. and J. Wang, *Relevance of big data to forensic accounting practice and education.* Managerial Auditing Journal, 2019. **34**(3): p. 268–288.
18. Alshurafat, H., et al. *The domain of forensic accounting services: evidence from Australia.* in *19th Asian Academic Accounting Association (FourA) Annual Conference*. 2019.
19. Alzahrane, M.A., *Insights from forensic accounting educators and practitioners within the KSA context regarding the optimal forensic accounting skills set: an implication on the socio-economic development.* Journal of Business and Socio-Economic Development, 2024. **4**(1): p. 66–80.
20. Alshurafat, H., M.O. Al Shbail, and E. Mansour, *Strengths and weaknesses of forensic accounting: an implication on the socio-economic development.* Journal of Business and Socio-economic Development, 2021.
21. Huber, W., *Forensic accountants, forensic accounting certifications, and due diligence.* Journal of Forensic & Investigative Accounting, 2013. **5**(1): p. 182–203.
22. Akinbowale, O.E., H.E. Klingelhöfer, and M.F. Zerihun, *Application of forensic accounting techniques in the South African banking industry for the purpose of fraud risk mitigation.* Cogent Economics & Finance, 2023. **11**(1): p. 2153412.
23. Akinbowale, O.E., H.E. Klingelhöfer, and M.F. Zerihun, *The integration of forensic accounting and the management control system as tools for combating cyberfraud.* Academy of Accounting and Financial Studies Journal, 2021. **25**(2): p. 1–14.

Chapter 2
Forensic Accounting Ethics: Authoritative Guidance and Non-Authoritative Guidance

2.1 Introduction

With the ongoing evolution of the business and industrial landscape, the frequency and complexity of ethical scandals and conflicts of interest have increased significantly. Such developments underscore the necessity of every profession being governed by a clear and comprehensive ethical code of conduct. An ethical code of conduct is not only a set of behavioral guidelines but also represents a key sociological dimension of professionalism, ensuring integrity, accountability, and public trust in professional practices [1–3].

Forensic accounting, as a specialized branch of the accounting profession, plays a critical role in investigating financial irregularities and providing expert testimony in legal disputes [4, 5]. Consequently, forensic accountants must possess a strong understanding of their ethical responsibilities and adhere to professional standards that guide their decision-making and conduct [6, 7]. However, in Jordan, there is currently no authoritative ethical framework that explicitly defines the responsibilities and moral values governing forensic accountants' work [2]. While some non-authoritative guidance is available through accounting-related bodies and governmental jurisdictions, it remains fragmented and lacks the formal recognition necessary to ensure consistency and professionalism in practice.

This chapter explores both authoritative and non-authoritative guidance relevant to forensic accounting practice in Jordan. It aims to highlight the ethical expectations placed on practitioners and to identify gaps in the current regulatory and professional landscape. Furthermore, as Alshurafat et al. [8] emphasize, educating future forensic accountants about ethical dilemmas requires experiential teaching approaches that simulate real-world professional scenarios. In line with this perspective, this paper also presents a set of hypothetical ethical situations (see Appendix) designed to enhance moral awareness and decision-making among forensic accounting students and practitioners.

H. Alshurafat, *Forensic Accounting*, https://doi.org/10.1007/978-981-95-8613-4_2

2.2 Ethical Values of the Forensic Accounting Profession: Prior Studies Evidence

Bologna and Lindquist [9] defined forensic accounting as the application of financial expertise and investigative skills within the rules of evidence. DiGabriele [10] emphasized that forensic accountants must possess knowledge of accounting, auditing, law, and investigation, complemented by ethical values and soft skills. While forensic accounting focuses on financial investigations, it also requires interrogative abilities, legal awareness, investigative proficiency, and interpersonal skills [11].

Many prior studies have discussed the ethical codes of conduct [12]. For example, Howieson [13] explored what constitutes good practice in forensic accounting by examining how virtue ethics might be relevant. Howieson stated that, since the forensic accounting profession is multidisciplinary, the required ethical principles might conflict with other legal compliance requirements. Moreover, there are several technical and personal characteristics relevant to a good forensic accountant; in other words, a forensic accountant must possess specific attributes to work ethically. The author affirmed that among these characteristics and attributes, practical wisdom is considered the most important in terms of maintaining public confidence and the quality of forensic accountant work.

Curtis [14] stated that ethics is an essential topic that should be provided to forensic accounting students, as forensic accountants face many ethical dilemmas. The literature indicates that most forensic accountants did not consider moral codes and standards before entering the profession [15]. This raises questions regarding forensic accountants' investigative ability. It raises further questions about forensic accountants' commitment to maintaining high ethical standards and professional practice standards. The results suggest a need for reform within the forensic certification industry: either the establishment of an independent agency to monitor and accredit forensic accounting corporations and their certifications, or the adoption of state or federal regulations to enforce minimum standards for forensic accounting corporations and their certifications. Huber [16] found that, while most forensic accountants practitioners believe it is essential for forensic accounting bodies to have a procedure for enforcing Ethical Codes of Conduct, many practitioners hold certifications from bodies that either do not have a Code of Ethics or do not have compliance procedures.

The American Institute of Certified Public Accountants suggested measures for forensic accounting ethical conduct, including (1) Forensic accountants should focus solely on reporting facts. (2) Forensic accountant practitioners must conduct themselves in an ethically way. (3) Forensic accountant practitioners should keep a good standard of the profession and not act on a monetary interest in any circumstance. (4) Forensic accountant practitioners should share the skills, experience, and knowledge with other colleagues in the field. (5) Forensic accountant practitioners should prevent conflicts of interest. (6) Forensic accountant practitioners should continue to improve through ongoing professional training. For Salleh and Ab Aziz [17], forensic accountants should uphold moral values aligned with Islamic sharia.

These top five Islamic ethical values rated and ranked as most important are: (1) Trustworthiness, (2) integrity (3) accountability (4) Transparency/honesty (5) discipline.

The following two tables summarize the literature on forensic accounting ethics. Table 2.1 summarizes the research topics, methodologies, and ethical lessons learned. Table 2.2 provides a thematic analysis of the results of forensic accounting ethics studies.

2.3 Ethical Code of Conduct for Forensic Accountants: From the Jordanian Perspective

The following are the laws, jurisdictions, and codes of conduct relevant to forensic accounting practitioners in the Jordanian context, with a short explanation of why each item matters in practice and how it typically applies to forensic work.

2.3.1 IESBA/International Code of Ethics, Adopted in Jordan via HCAP/JACPA

The International Ethics Standards Board for Accountants (IESBA) Code of Ethics is the global principles-based ethics standard (integrity, objectivity, professional competence & due care, confidentiality, professional behaviour). Jordan's Higher Council for the Accountancy Profession (HCAP) and the Jordanian Association of Certified Public Accountants (JACPA) have adopted the IESBA Code; revisions from IESBA apply in Jordan. JACPA members (and generally recognised professional accountants in Jordan) must follow IESBA principles when performing forensic engagements. These principles govern conflicts of interest, independence, confidentiality, and professional competence in investigative tasks.[1]

2.3.2 Jordan Integrity & Anti-Corruption Law/Integrity & Anti-Corruption Commission (JIACC)

The Integrity and Anti-Corruption Law (initially Law No. 62 of 2006, with subsequent amendments) and the Commission (JIACC) set out corruption offences, prevention measures, and investigative powers. Forensic accountants often support corruption investigations (e.g., evidence gathering and tracing illicit flows). JIACC's

[1] https://www.ifac.org/about-ifac/membership/members/jordanian-association-certified-public-accountants?utm

Table 2.1 Summary of forensic accounting ethics studies

Author(s) & year	Focus of study	Context	Methodology	Key findings	Ethical issues addressed	Implications for forensic accounting practice
Crumbley and Heitger [18]	Forensic and Investigative Accounting	USA	Conceptual/ Textbook	Establishes forensic accounting as a blend of auditing, law, and ethics	Independence, integrity, objectivity	Ethics should be a formal component of professional certification programs
Digabriele [10]	An Empirical Investigation of the Relevant Skills of Forensic Accountants	USA	Quantitative/ Survey	Ethics and communication are rated as essential competencies	Integrity, professional skepticism	Ethical acumen is a distinguishing skill for forensic accountants versus auditors
Huber [19]	Forensic Accounting, Fraud Theory, and the Ethics of Fraud Investigation	USA	Conceptual/ Theoretical	Critiques ethical dilemmas in investigative practice	Bias, due process, objectivity	Calls for explicit ethical frameworks for investigative work
Curtis [14]	Are Ethical Decisions Dependent upon Mood?	USA	Experimental	Emotional states impact ethical judgment accuracy	Emotional bias	Emphasizes emotional awareness in ethics training
Kranacher and Riley [20]	Forensic Accounting and Fraud Examination	USA	Case-based/ Educational	Advocates for ethics as a pillar in anti-fraud education	Confidentiality, conflicts of interest	Ethics instruction must be embedded in all forensic courses
Davis et al. [21]	Characteristics and Skills of the Forensic Accountant	USA	Descriptive/ Survey	Ethical conduct consistently ranked above technical skills	Objectivity, honesty	Hiring standards should prioritize ethical reputation
Enofe et al. [22]	Forensic Accounting and Fraud Detection in Nigeria	Nigeria	Quantitative	Links ethical practices to successful fraud detection	Corruption, lack of transparency	Strong ethical regulation enhances forensic effectiveness
Ozili [23]	Ethics and Accountability in Forensic Accounting Practice	Global	Conceptual/ Critical review	Reframes forensic ethics as public accountability	Public trust, transparency	Forensic ethics must address social responsibility
Adeosun and Owolabi [24]	Forensic Accounting and Ethical Responsibility	Nigeria	Empirical/ Survey	Ethical commitment predicts effectiveness	Diligence, accountability	Promotes ethical training and regulatory enforcement
Owolabi et al. [25]	Artificial Intelligence and Ethical Challenges in Forensic Accounting	Global	Conceptual/ Emerging issues	Explores ethical dilemmas in AI-driven forensic investigations	Data privacy, bias, accountability	Calls for new ethical frameworks addressing AI-assisted investigations

Table 2.2 Thematic analysis of the results of forensic accounting ethics studies

Theme	Summary insights
Ethics as Core Competence	Ethics is consistently identified as a key professional skill for forensic accountants
Institutional Weakness and Ethics	Developing nations face greater ethical lapses due to weak institutions
Education and Training	Ethics training improves judgment and reduces misconduct
Emotional and Cognitive Biases	Personal mood and bias influence ethical decision-making
Technology and Ethics	Emerging digital tools pose new ethical challenges
Public Accountability	Ethics are linked to restoring trust in financial systems

remit, reporting channels, whistle-blower protections, and sanctions create the legal framework within which forensic evidence may be submitted or used.[2]

2.3.3 *Anti-Money-Laundering & Counter-Terrorist-Financing (AML/CFT) Law & AMLU (Financial Intelligence Unit)*

Jordan's AML/CFT framework (Law No. 46/2007 and subsequent consolidated/amended versions, most recently Law No. 20/2021 and other amendments) and the AML Unit (AMLU) set obligations for suspicious transaction reporting, customer due diligence (CDD/KYC), record-keeping, and sanctions. Forensic accountants working on money laundering, asset tracing, or compliance reviews must follow AML rules, report suspicious activities through the AMLU where required, and may be called to provide expert analysis in AML prosecutions or administrative actions.[3]

2.3.4 *Companies Law (No. 22/1997) and Amendments (Including Law No. 19/2021 and Later Updates)*

Jordan's principal corporate law (with amendments) regulates company formation, director duties, financial disclosure, and, since recent amendments, beneficial ownership disclosure and other governance measures. Forensic accountants routinely examine corporate records, related-party transactions, and beneficial-ownership structures. Companies Law provisions on director duties, disclosure, and potential

[2] https://www.jiacc.gov.jo/En/Pages/About_the_Authority?utm

[3] chromeextension://efaidnbmnnnibpcajpcglclefindmkaj/; https://www.amlu.gov.jo/ebv4.0/root_storage/en/eb_list_page/law_no.%2846%29_for_2007___anti_money_laundering_and_counter_terrorist_financing_law..pdf?utm.com

criminal penalties give forensic findings legal relevance and can trigger regulatory or criminal follow-up.[4]

2.3.5 *Penal Code/Criminal Law (Fraud, Embezzlement, Falsification Offences)*

Jordanian criminal statutes define offences such as fraud, embezzlement, forgery, and related crimes; these statutes determine the elements of offences and potential criminal liability. (Relevant texts are published in the Official Gazette and consolidated legal sources.)Forensic accountants provide evidence that maps to statutory elements (e.g., proving intent, false accounting entries, misappropriation). Prosecutors and courts often use their reports to establish the legal aspects of a crime.[5]

2.3.6 *Central Bank of Jordan (CBJ) Rules & Banking Law/ Sectoral Regulations*

CBJ regulations and banking laws set AML/CFT obligations for banks, confidentiality and data-handling rules, reporting channels, and supervisory powers. The CBJ issues circulars and compliance expectations for financial institutions. Forensic accountants working on bank records, transactional tracing, or bank compliance reviews must understand CBJ requirements and the treatment of bank secrecy versus legal reporting obligations.[6]

2.3.7 *Jordan Securities Commission (JSC Rules & Corporate Governance Code)*

The JSC supervises capital markets, disclosure rules for listed companies, and corporate governance requirements; it also enforces market-related offences. Forensic work involving listed entities (insider trading, financial statement manipulation, market abuse) will interface with JSC investigations and evidentiary standards.[7]

[4] Natlex+1.

[5] *(local penal code texts and official consolidated laws are available through Jordanian government legal resources and legal databases, see JIACC/OECD analyses for context).* UNODC+1.

[6] orient-lawfirm.com

[7] FATF+1.

2.3.8 Regulatory/Professional Frameworks & Oversight Bodies

HCAP (Higher Council for the Accountancy Profession) and JACPA (Jordanian Association of Certified Public Accountants) regulate professional conduct, licensing, inspections, and adoption of international standards (IFRS, ISAs, IESBA). The JACPA has inspection and disciplinary powers for auditors and can recommend rules to HCAP. Forensic accountants who are licensed/regulated must meet professional competence, quality control, and disciplinary standards; JACPA/HCAP guidance affects reporting standards, peer review, and sanctions for ethical breaches.[8] In accordance with Accountancy Profession Law No. 73 of 2003, the Jordanian Association of Certified Public Accountants (JACPA) and the Higher Council for the Accountancy Profession (HCAP) specify applicable ethical standards in Jordan. JACPA is responsible for recommending the ethical standards for HCAP to adopt. In 1992, HCAP adopted the IESBA Code of Ethics for all Professional Accountants in Jordan. All revised and new requirements of the IESBA Code are applicable in Jordan, with effect from the IESBA's effective date. The International Arab Society of Certified Accountants (IASCA) offers voluntary designations and requires its members to adhere to the latest version of the IESBA Code of Ethics.[9]

2.3.9 International Conventions and Regional Instruments

Jordan is party to regional/international instruments (e.g., the Arab Convention on Transnational Organized Crime and UNCAC obligations), and FATF/MENAFATF assessments inform national law and practice. OECD and MENAFATF reports note Jordan's evolving integrity framework. International obligations shape domestic enforcement priorities (anti-corruption, asset recovery, mutual legal assistance) and, therefore, the context in which forensic accountants operate in cross-border cases.[10]

2.3.10 Evidence, Criminal Procedure, and Court Practice Rules

Jordan's rules on admissibility of documentary and expert evidence, chain of custody, witness testimony, and expert reports (found in procedural codes and court practice) determine how forensic accounting evidence must be prepared and presented.Forensic reports must conform to evidentiary standards (clear methodology,

[8] ifacweb.blob.core.windows.net+1.

[9] https://www.ifac.org/about-ifac/membership/profile/jordan

[10] FATF+1.

chain of custody, transparency of assumptions) for admissibility and weight in court proceedings.

Table 2.3 highlights how ethical principles are operationalized under Jordanian law and professional codes.

In summary, the ethical framework for forensic accountants in Jordan requires maintaining the following:

- Integrity
- Objectivity and Independence
- Professional Competence and Due Care
- Confidentiality and Data Protection
- Accountability and Public Interest Responsibility
- Legal and Regulatory Compliance
- Professional Behavior
- Transparency and Cooperation
- International Ethical Alignment

2.4 International Ethical Codes of Conducts

Table 2.4 presents a comparative summary of the core ethical principles guiding accountants and forensic practitioners under various professional codes of ethics across different jurisdictions. Despite minor terminological variations, these frameworks share a common foundation built upon integrity, objectivity, professional competence, confidentiality, responsibility, and professional behavior. The six universal pillars of ethical conduct in the forensic accounting profession.

Figure 2.1 shows the definition of each one of the universal pillars of ethical conduct in the forensic accounting profession.

2.5 Conclusion

In this chapter, both authoritative and non-authoritative ethical principles and codes of conduct relevant to forensic accounting practice have been reviewed and analyzed. The discussion included an overview of the existing literature on forensic accounting ethics, highlighting current discourse and research trends in ethical behavior in the profession. Furthermore, the chapter examined the ethical and professional frameworks that apply to forensic accountants within both the Jordanian and international contexts, emphasizing the importance of aligning local practice with global standards.

The review revealed that the core ethical principles that forensic accountants must uphold include: integrity; objectivity and independence; professional competence and due care; confidentiality and data protection; accountability and public interest responsibility; legal and regulatory compliance; professional behavior; transparency and cooperation; and international ethical alignment. These principles collectively provide the moral foundation necessary for ensuring professionalism, credibility, and public trust in forensic accounting practice.

Table 2.3 Practical implications for forensic accountants in Jordan

Area of ethical/ legal obligation	Required actions for forensic accountants	Relevant legislation/code
Professional Ethics & Integrity	Adhere to principles of integrity, objectivity, confidentiality, competence, and professional behavior. Maintain independence and avoid conflicts of interest	IESBA Code of Ethics (adopted by JACPA/HCAP)
Anti-Money Laundering (AML) Compliance	Conduct due diligence, monitor transactions, and report suspicious activities to the Anti-Money Laundering Unit (AMLU). Maintain proper documentation and training in AML/CFT procedures	AML/CFT Law No. 46 of 2007 and amendments (Law No. 20 of 2021)
Anti-Corruption & Integrity Standards	Identify and report indicators of corruption or fraud; cooperate with JIACC investigations. Uphold transparency and accountability in engagements	Integrity and Anti-Corruption Law No. 62 of 2006 (and amendments); JIACC Regulations
Corporate Governance & Disclosure	Examine compliance with corporate laws, beneficial ownership, and directors' duties. Report irregularities objectively in accordance with statutory requirements	Companies Law No. 22 of 1997 (amended 2021); JSC Corporate Governance Code
Criminal Law & Evidence Requirements	Ensure all findings comply with Jordanian evidentiary standards, maintain proper chain of custody, and document analytical methods. Prepare expert reports suitable for judicial proceedings	Jordanian Penal Code; Criminal Procedure Code
Banking & Financial Sector Regulations	Respect confidentiality and data-access rules when working with financial institutions. Understand reporting channels under CBJ and AML regulations	Central Bank of Jordan (CBJ) Instructions; Banking Law
Securities & Capital Market Investigations	Apply forensic techniques in detecting insider trading, financial statement manipulation, or securities fraud. Align findings with regulatory standards	Jordan Securities Commission (JSC) Regulations
Confidentiality & Data Protection	Safeguard all confidential information obtained during investigations. Disclose only when legally required or authorized	IESBA Code; Jordanian Penal Code (confidentiality clauses)
International & Regional Cooperation	Follow international best practices and obligations under UNCAC, FATF, and MENAFATF frameworks for cross-border forensic investigations	UNCAC (ratified by Jordan in 2005); MENAFATF Recommendations

Table 2.4 Ethical principles among international ethical codes of conducts

Organization/country	Ethical principles
AICPA (USA)	• Responsibility • Public interest • Integrity • Objectivity • Due care • Confidentiality *Strongly emphasizes the public interest in ethical dilemmas
IFAC/IESBA (International)	• Integrity • Objectivity • Professional competence due care • Confidentiality • Professional behavior
Accountancy Europe (EU)	• Integrity • Objectivity • Professional competence due care • Confidentiality • Professional behavior
JICPA (Japan)	• Integrity • Objectivity • Professional competence due care • Confidentiality • Professional behavior
APES/Australia APES 215	• Conflicts of interest • Independence • Reporting integrity • Confidentiality • Responsibility * Specific guidance for expert witnesses
CPA Canada (Canada)	• Professional behavior • Integrity and due care • Objectivity • Confidentiality *Highlights public trust and transparency in reporting; includes specific guidance for expert witnesses
SAICA/IRBA (South Africa)	• Integrity • Objectivity • Professional competence and due care • Confidentiality • Professional behavior *Adds focus on public accountability and anti-corruption ethics within forensic audits
ICAI (India)	• Integrity • Independence • Professional competence • Confidentiality • Objectivity *Emphasizes independence and anti-fraud responsibility under India's Companies Act reforms

(continued)

Table 2.4 (continued)

Organization/country	Ethical principles
ICAN (Nigeria)	• Integrity • Objectivity • Professional competence and due care • Confidentiality • Professional behavior *Aligns with IFAC; stresses accountability and transparency in public-sector engagements
CMA/CPA (Bangladesh & Pakistan)	• Integrity • Objectivity • Professional competence • Confidentiality • Professional behavior *Reinforces ethics in anti-corruption and forensic financial reporting initiatives

Sources: Adapted from AICPA [26], IESBA [27], Accountancy Europe [28], JICPA [29], APES 215 [30], SAICA [31], ICAI [32], ICAN [33], CPA Canada [34], and Işik [35]

Appendix: Ethical Situations

These four examples together create a coherent semester-long journaling framework, touching on major ethical themes in forensic accounting:

1. Conflicts of interest
2. Integrity and transparency
3. Bribery and professional independence
4. Whistleblowing and moral courage

Example 1
Samir discovers that Layla, a junior accountant on his team, is a close friend with the foundation's finance director. Layla insists that her personal relationship will not interfere with her professional judgment and refuses to step aside from the case.

Questions to Consider:

- What ethical issues arise from Layla's situation?
- How should Dr. Samir respond to maintain objectivity and independence?
- Which ethical principles (e.g., integrity, objectivity, professional behavior) apply according to the IFAC or AICPA codes?
- If you were in Layla's position, what would you do, and why?

Example 2
Samir uncovers evidence that the foundation's director, Khalid, has approved small "administrative bonuses" for himself and several board members. When confronted,

Integrity	• Integrity refers to being honest, straightforward, and fair in all professional and business relationships. It means adhering to moral and ethical principles even when under pressure or when no one is watching.
Objectivity	• Objectivity is the obligation to avoid bias, conflict of interest, or undue influence that may compromise professional judgment.
Professional Competence and Due Care	• Professional competence and due care require accountants to maintain professional knowledge and skill at a level necessary to provide competent services, and to act diligently in accordance with applicable technical and professional standards.
Confidentiality	• Confidentiality requires professionals to protect sensitive information acquired during the course of their work and not to disclose it without proper authority or legal duty.
Accountability and Public Interest Responsibility	• Responsibility means being accountable for one's professional actions and decisions, recognizing the duty to act in the public interest and uphold the credibility of the profession.
Professional Behavior	• Professional behavior requires accountants to comply with laws and regulations and to avoid any conduct that discredits the profession.
Legal and Regulatory Compliance	• The obligation of forensic accountants to act in accordance with all applicable laws, regulations, and professional standards governing financial investigations and reporting.
Transparency and Cooperation	• The ethical duty of forensic accountants to conduct their work openly, communicate findings clearly, and collaborate effectively with oversight authorities and stakeholders involved in investigations.
International Ethical Alignment	• ensuring that forensic accounting practices and ethical conduct in Jordan are consistent with internationally recognized standards and conventions governing integrity, anti-corruption, and financial transparency.

Fig. 2.1 Six universal pillars of ethical conduct in the forensic accounting profession: definitions

Khalid argues that exposing the issue could harm the foundation's reputation and reduce future donations. He asks Samir to "let it go" for the greater good.

Questions to Consider:

- Should Dr. Samir report the findings despite the potential harm to the foundation's image? Why or why not?
- How might teleological ethics (outcome-based) versus deontological ethics (duty-based) guide his decision?
- What responsibilities does a forensic accountant have to the public, the client, and the profession?
- How would you handle this situation to balance ethical integrity with compassion?

Example 3

As the investigation deepens, Samir learns that one of the foundation's suppliers, Nadia Trading Co., has been inflating invoice amounts. When he approaches the company's accountant for clarification, the accountant discreetly offers Samir a "gift"—a gold watch—in appreciation for his "understanding" and cooperation.

Questions to Consider:

- What ethical principles are being challenged in this situation?
- Should Dr. Samir accept or reject the gift? Why?
- How should he report or document this interaction according to professional standards?
- Would your response change if refusing the gift could jeopardize access to key evidence or cooperation from the supplier? Explain your reasoning.

Example 4

One of Samir's assistants, Omar, uncovers digital evidence suggesting that a member of the foundation's board has been diverting funds to a private account. Before Omar can finalize his report, an anonymous email warns him to "be careful" and suggests that making the findings public could endanger both his safety and the firm's reputation.

Questions to Consider:

- What ethical and professional duties does Omar have in this situation?
- How should Dr. Samir support his assistant while ensuring the integrity of the investigation?
- How do justice ethics and virtue ethics apply here?
- If you were in Omar's position, would you proceed with the report? Why or why not?

References

1. Alshurafat, H., *Forensic accounting as a profession in Australia? A sociological perspective.* Meditari Accountancy Research, 2021.
2. Almashaqbeh, R.N., H. Alshurafat, and H. Al Amosh, *The Impact of Professionalism Theory Constructs on the Applicability of Forensic Accounting Services: Evidence from Jordan.* International Journal of Financial Studies, 2023. **11**(4): p. 141.
3. Huber, W., *Is forensic accounting in the United States becoming a profession?* Journal of Forensic & Investigative Accounting, 2012. **4**(1).
4. Ismail, S., R.M. Abdou, and M.S. Ibrahim, *Who is Better in Practicing Customer Due Diligence as an Anti-Money Laundering Tool for Financial Institutions: Can Internal Auditors Be Forensic Accountants? Evidence from the MENA Region*, in *Sustainable Data Management: Navigating Big Data, Communication Technology, and Business Digital Leadership. Volume 1*. 2025, Springer. p. 11–23.
5. Ahmad, S., M.S. Ibrahim, and R.M. Abdou, *Understanding the Role of Forensic Accountants in Due Diligence Within Organizations and Its Impact on Organizational Learning.* Sustainable Data Management: Navigating Big Data, Communication Technology, and Business Digital Leadership. Volume 1, 2025: p. 3–10.
6. Alkababji, M.W., et al., *Forensic Accounting Practices: Evaluating the Current Research*, in *Achieving Sustainable Business Through AI, Technology Education and Computer Science: Volume 3: Business Sustainability and Artificial Intelligence Applications.* 2024, Springer. p. 767–777.
7. Guellim, N., et al., *Evaluating the perceived value of forensic accounting: a systematic review method.* Discover Sustainability, 2024. **5**(1): p. 351.
8. Alshurafat, H., et al., *Perceptions of the usefulness of various teaching methods in forensic accounting education.* Accounting Education, 2020. **29**(2): p. 177–204.
9. Bologna, J. and R.J. Lindquist, *Fraud auditing and forensic accounting: new tools and techniques.* 1995: John Wiley & Sons Inc.
10. DiGabriele, J.A., *An empirical investigation of the relevant skills of forensic accountants.* Journal of Education for Business, 2008. **83**(6): p. 331–338.
11. DiGabriele, J.A., *Combining elements of the fraud triangle and professional skepticism in the valuation of lost profits.* 2009.
12. Al-Raggad, M., et al., *Unveiling financial crimes: advancing forensic accounting practices and ethical integrity through bibliometric insights.* Safer Communities, 2025. **24**(3): p. 244–264.
13. Howieson, B., *What is the 'good'forensic accountant? A virtue ethics perspective.* Pacific Accounting Review, 2018. **30**(2): p. 155–167.
14. Curtis, G.E., *Legal and regulatory environments and ethics: Essential components of a fraud and forensic accounting curriculum.* Issues in Accounting Education, 2008. **23**(4): p. 535.
15. Huber, D., *Forensic accounting corporations' codes of ethics and standards of practice–a comparison.* International Journal of Accounting, Auditing and Performance Evaluation, 2013. **9**(2): p. 126–152.
16. Huber, D., *Forensic accountants, codes of ethics, and forensic accounting corporations.* Journal of Forensic Studies in Accounting and Business, 2013. **5**(1): p. 70–101.
17. Salleh, K. and R. Ab Aziz, *Traits, skills and ethical values of public sector forensic accountants: an empirical investigation.* Procedia-Social and Behavioral Sciences, 2014. **145**: p. 361–370.
18. Crumbley, D. and L. Heitger, *Smith, GS (2013).* Forensic and investigative accounting.
19. Huber, W. D., Forensic accounting, fraud theory, and the end of the fraud triangle. Journal of Theoretical Accounting Research, 2017. **12**(2): p. 28–48.
20. Kranacher, M. and J. Riley, *RA i WELLS, JT (2011.) Forensic Accounting and Fraud Examination. Hoboken.* New Jersey: John Wiley & Sons, Inc.

21. Davis, C., R. Farrell, and S. Ogilby, *Characteristics and skills of the Forensic Accountant.* American Institute of Certified Public Accountants, 2010: p. 11–26.
22. Enofe, A., P. Omagbon, and F. Ehigiator, *Forensic audit and corporate fraud.* IIARD International Journal of Economics and Business Management, 2015. **1**(7): p. 1–10.
23. Ozili, P.K., *Forensic accounting theory*, in *Uncertainty and Challenges in Contemporary Economic Behaviour*. 2020, Emerald Publishing Limited.
24. Adeosun, O.T. and K.E. Owolabi, *Gender inequality: determinants and outcomes in Nigeria.* Journal of Business and Socio-economic Development, 2021.
25. Owolabi, A., et al., *Understanding the Adoption of AI in Accounting and Finance in Emerging Economies—Insights from the Banking and Finance Sector*, in *The Impact of Artificial Intelligence on Finance: Transforming Financial Technologies*. 2025, Springer. p. 111–126.
26. American Institute of Certified Public Accountants, Enhancing audit quality: Plans and perspectives for the U.S. audit profession. 2014, New York, NY: AICPA.
27. International Ethics Standards Board for Accountants, Handbook of the International Code of Ethics for Professional Accountants (including International Independence Standards). 2022, New York, NY: International Federation of Accountants.
28. Accountancy Europe, Ethics and independence in auditing: Emerging challenges for the profession. 2025, Brussels: Accountancy Europe.
29. Japanese Institute of Certified Public Accountants, Code of Ethics for Professional Accountants. 2020, Tokyo: JICPA.
30. Accounting Professional & Ethical Standards Board, PES 215: Forensic Accounting Services. 2019, Melbourne: APESB.
31. South African Institute of Chartered Accountants, Code of Professional Conduct. 2021, Johannesburg: SAICA.
32. Institute of Chartered Accountants of India, Code of Ethics. 2022, New Delhi: ICAI.
33. Institute of Chartered Accountants of Nigeria, ICAN Code of Ethics and Professional Conduct. 2023, Lagos: ICAN.
34. Chartered Professional Accountants of Canada, CPA Code of Professional Conduct. 2022, Toronto: CPA Canada.
35. Işik, B.K., *ETHICS IN FORENSIC ACCOUNTING: CHALLENGES, IMPACTS AND FUTURE DIRECTIONS*. Anadolu Üniversitesi İktisadi ve İdari Bilimler Fakültesi Dergisi, 2025. **26**(3): p. 316–337.

Chapter 3
Forensic Accounting Role in Fraud Investigation, Prevention, and Mitigation

3.1 Introduction

Recently, cases of fraud have increased significantly. The harmful effects of fraud have impacted individuals, companies, and governments alike [1–3]. According to a recent study by the Association of Certified Fraud Examiners (ACFE), the estimated loss from occupational fraud alone is $3.1 billion. Organisations worldwide are believed to lose around 5% of their annual revenue to fraud, with the average loss per case at $1.7 million and the median at $145,000.

Forensic accountants are recognised for their expertise, skills, and abilities in detecting and preventing fraud. Practitioners in forensic accounting can investigate various types of fraud, including occupational fraud, one-to-one fraud, and other financial crimes.

In this chapter, the types of fraud and financial crimes are defined and illustrated with examples, along with the statistical and accounting techniques forensic accountants use to detect fraud. Moreover, this chapter highlights the negative impact of fraud on business and concludes by offering implications for practitioners and regulators in the field of fraud.

3.2 What Is Fraud?

According to Black's Law Dictionary, fraud is defined as "any activity that relies on deception in order to achieve a gain".[1] Albrecht et al. [4] stated that fraud is a "generic term, and embraces all the multifarious means which human ingenuity can devise, which are resorted to by one individual, to get an advantage over another by

[1] https://www.acfe.com/fraud-resources/fraud-101-what-is-fraud

H. Alshurafat, *Forensic Accounting*, https://doi.org/10.1007/978-981-95-8613-4_3

false representations. No definite and invariable rule can be laid down as a general proposition in defining fraud, as it includes surprise, trickery, cunning, and unfair ways by which another is cheated. The only boundaries defining it are those which limit human knavery." Based on the above-mentioned definitions and discussions, fraud elements could include the following:

A. a fraudulent or a fraud group.
B. deception matter (could be an idea, a product, or a combination of them).
C. a victim or group of victims.

3.3 Fraud Tree

To classify fraud types, prior researchers often use the fraud tree, which classifies fraud into three major categories: occupational fraud, external fraud, and individual fraud, as shown in Fig. 3.1 [6, 7].

3.3.1 Occupational Fraud

In terms of occupational fraud, the ACFE publishes the Occupational Fraud: A Report to the Nations, which shows the most common types of occupational fraud, along with yearly statistics on the cost and frequency of fraud cases. In this report, the ACFE classifies fraud cases using the fraud tree shown in Fig. 3.2.

Each type of occupational fraud includes subtypes. However, it is important to define each type to understand its nature, schemes, and impact fully.

3.3.1.1 Corruption

Corruption refers to the misuse of authority to obtain unlawful benefits that are not aligned with the organisation's interests. According to Jain [8], corruption is defined as "the acts in which the power of public offices is used for personal gains in a manner that contravenes the rules of the game." Corruption schemes may include, for example, conflicts of interest, bribery, illegal gratuities, and economic extortion. Table 3.1 provides definitions and hypothetical examples for each scheme.

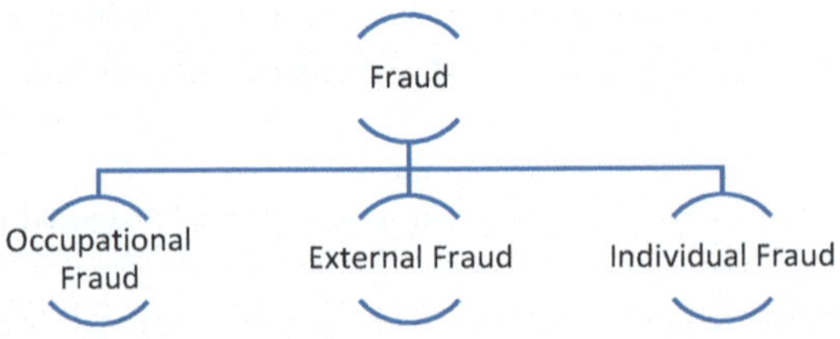

Fig. 3.1 First-level fraud tree. Source: Adopted from Crain et al. [5]

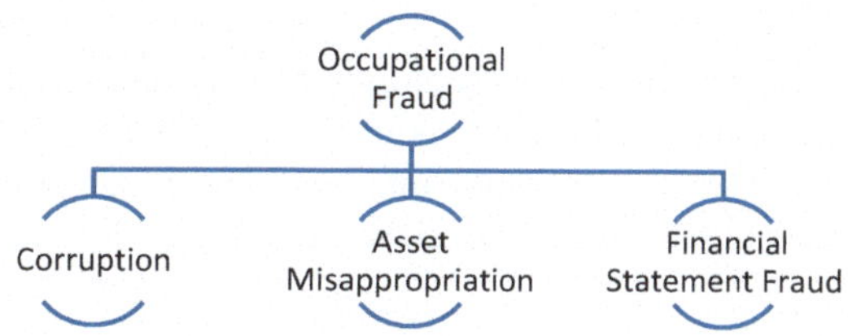

Fig. 3.2 Occupational fraud tree. Source: adopted from Occupational Fraud 2024: A Report to the Nations

Table 3.1 Corruption scheme schemes, definitions, and hypothetical examples

Corruption scheme	Definition	Hypothetical example
Conflicts of Interest	Occurs when an employee or public official has an undisclosed personal or financial interest that may improperly influence their professional decisions	A government purchasing officer awards a contract to a construction company owned by their brother without disclosing their relationship
Bribery	The offering, giving, receiving, or soliciting of something of value to influence an official act or decision	A supplier pays a company manager $10,000 to ensure their bid is selected for a new supply contract
Illegal Gratuities	A reward or gift given to an employee or official for an act that has already been performed, often as a "thank you" for favorable treatment	After approving a vendor's permit, a city inspector receives an expensive watch as a gesture of appreciation from the vendor
Economic Extortion	When someone demands payment or another benefit under threat (explicit or implied) to take or withhold an action that affects another person or entity	A customs officer threatens to delay the shipment of goods unless the importer pays a "facilitation fee"
Invoice Kickbacks	A form of bribery in which an employee receives a payment ("kickback") from a vendor for approving inflated or fake invoices	A procurement officer approves a supplier's overpriced invoice and receives a 10% cash kickback
Bid Rigging	Collusion among vendors or between vendors and employees to manipulate the outcome of a competitive bidding process	An insider shares competitors' bids with a preferred vendor to ensure the preferred vendor submits the winning bid

3.3.1.2 Asset Misappropriation

Assets misappropriation is defined as "the improper conversion of an asset for personal use" [5]. According to the 2024 Occupational Fraud Report to the Nations, asset misappropriation varies widely in cost and scope. It accounts for 89% of fraud cases. The schemes involved in asset misappropriation can take many forms, including cash-related frauds such as fraudulent disbursements, theft of cash on hand, theft of cash receipts, skimming, and cash larceny. They may also involve manipulating financial transactions, such as falsified sales or shipping records, refunds and write-offs, register disbursements, and tampering with checks or payments. In some instances, employees commit billing or payroll fraud, such as creating fictitious (ghost) employees, falsifying wage records, submitting false expense reports, or claiming multiple reimbursements. Other examples include using company assets or inventory for personal purchases, creating shell companies or fictitious vendors to divert funds, or engaging in forgery and check alteration. Overall, these schemes aim to conceal the diversion of funds or assets through falsified records, unauthorised transactions, or the misuse of legitimate processes [9]. Table 3.2 presents a definition and a hypothetical example for each scheme.

3.3.1.3 Financial Statements Fraud

Financial statements fraud involves deliberately manipulating an organisation's financial records to present a distorted view of its economic performance or position. It can take many forms, usually aimed at overstating success or hiding problems. Common types include conflicts of interest, in which employees or executives act in their own interests rather than the company's. Purchasing schemes, invoice kickbacks, and sales schemes are also common. Fraudsters may additionally alter accounting records to mislead stakeholders [10]. This includes overstating or understating income and net worth, recording fictitious revenues, concealing liabilities and expenses, improperly valuing assets, or making false or incomplete disclosures. Timing differences may also be employed, such as recording revenues too early or delaying expenses to make financial results appear stronger [11, 12]. Table 3.3 provides definitions and hypothetical examples for each scheme.

3.3.2 External Fraud

Organizations are exposed to a wide range of fraud schemes within their external environment [13–15]. According to [5], vendor fraud, competitor fraud, and client fraud are the common types of external fraud that organizations face (see Fig. 3.3). Table 3.4 provides definitions and hypothetical examples of each scheme.

3.3.2.1 Vendor Fraud

Vendors, in general, are not able to commit fraud against organizations with sophisticated and successful purchasing professionals. The main factor found to influence vendor fraud is the weakness of internal controls [16]. Among different types of vendor fraud, the most common schemes are short shipments, balance billing, and fraudulent cost-plus billing. Table 3.4 provides definitions and hypothetical examples of each scheme.

Table 3.2 Asset misappropriation schemes, definitions, and hypothetical examples

Scheme type	Definition	Hypothetical example
Cash Fraudulent Disbursements	The intentional issuing of payments for false, inflated, or unauthorized purposes	An employee creates a fake invoice and processes a payment to a non-existent supplier, depositing the funds into their personal account
Theft of Cash Receipts	Stealing cash that the organization has received but not yet recorded in the accounting system	A cashier pockets customer payments before entering them into the register
Theft of Cash on Hand	Taking physical cash directly from the company's cash reserves or petty cash fund	An office administrator removes $500 from the petty cash box and falsifies records to conceal the shortage
Asset Requisitions and Transfers	Misusing the organization's asset request or transfer process to divert assets for personal use	An employee requests new computer equipment "for another department" but takes it home for personal use
False Sales and Shipping	Recording fictitious sales or shipments to conceal stolen inventory or inflate performance	A warehouse clerk records a sale and shipment to a fake customer, then sells the goods privately
Purchasing and Receiving Schemes	Manipulating the procurement or receiving process to obtain unauthorized goods or payments	A purchasing agent orders extra materials and arranges for the excess to be delivered to their home
Unconcealed Larceny	Openly stealing company property without attempting to hide the theft through accounting manipulation	A warehouse worker takes tools home after work and uses them for personal business
Register Disbursements	Recording false transactions at a cash register to conceal stolen funds	A cashier processes a false refund and keeps the refunded cash
Check and Payment Tampering	Altering or forging checks or electronic payments to redirect funds for personal gain	An accountant changes the payee name on a company check to their own name before depositing it
Expense Reimbursement Schemes	Submitting false or inflated expense claims for personal reimbursement	An employee submits receipts for a personal vacation and labels them as a business trip
Payroll Schemes	Manipulating payroll systems to receive unauthorized compensation	A payroll clerk creates a "ghost employee" and pays them a salary
Billing Schemes	Creating or manipulating invoices to receive improper payments	An employee sets up a company and bills their employer for fake consulting services
Cash Larceny	Stealing cash after it has been recorded but before it is deposited	A store manager removes $200 from daily deposits before taking them to the bank
Skimming	Stealing incoming cash before it is recorded in the organization's books	A salesperson keeps part of a customer's cash payment and records a lower sale amount

(continued)

Table 3.2 (continued)

Scheme type	Definition	Hypothetical example
Sales Receivables and Refunds Schemes	Misappropriating funds by issuing false refunds or credit adjustments	A clerk issues a fake refund to a friend's credit card and splits the money
Lapping Schemes	Using payments from one customer to cover stolen payments from another to conceal theft	An accounts receivable clerk steals a payment from Customer A and uses Customer B's payment to hide the shortage
Fake Company Schemes	Creating a fake company to bill the organization for non-existent goods or services	An employee sets up a fictitious vendor and submits invoices for "marketing services"
Non-Accomplice Vendor Schemes	Diverting legitimate payments intended for real vendors to personal accounts	A fraudster changes a vendor's bank details in the system to their own account
Personal Purchases	Using company funds or accounts to buy personal items	A manager uses the company credit card to buy home appliances
Ghost Employee Schemes	Adding fictitious employees to the payroll and collecting their salaries	A payroll clerk enters a fake employee record and directs payments to their own account
Falsified Wages	Inflating hours worked or pay rates to receive extra compensation	An employee falsifies time sheets to claim overtime never worked
Commission Schemes	Manipulating sales records to receive unearned commissions	A salesperson records fake sales to earn higher commission bonuses
False Voids	Recording voided transactions to conceal theft of cash from the register	A cashier voids legitimate sales and keeps the customer's payment
False Refunds	Issuing fake refunds to cover up cash theft	A store employee processes a refund for a product that was never returned and keeps the money
Mischaracterized Expenses	Claiming personal costs as legitimate business expenses	An employee labels a family dinner as a "client meeting" and submits it for reimbursement
Overstated Expenses	Inflating actual expenses to obtain higher reimbursements	A staff member claims $300 for a hotel stay that actually cost $150
Fictitious Expenses	Submitting claims for expenses that were never incurred	An employee fabricates a taxi receipt for a trip that never occurred
Multiple Reimbursements	Submitting the same expense multiple times for reimbursement	An employee sends the same hotel invoice to both their manager and HR, resulting in double payment
Forged Maker Scheme	Forging an authorized signature on a company check	A bookkeeper signs a company check using the CFO's forged signature
Forged Endorsement Scheme	Stealing and endorsing a check meant for another party	An employee intercepts a vendor's check and signs it over to themselves
Altered Payee Scheme	Changing the name of the check recipient after it's issued	An accountant alters a check originally made out to "ABC Supplies" and pays it to themselves

(continued)

Table 3.2 (continued)

Scheme type	Definition	Hypothetical example
Authorized Maker Scheme	Using legitimate authority to issue fraudulent checks	A finance officer writes a check to a personal account but records it as a business expense

Table 3.3 Financial statements fraud schemes, definitions, and hypothetical examples

Scheme type	Definition	Hypothetical example
Conflicts of Interest	Occurs when an employee or executive uses their position to benefit personally rather than acting in the company's best interest	A general manager acts in a way that maximizes his own compensation rather than the owner's wealth
Purchasing Schemes	Manipulating purchasing or procurement processes for personal or financial advantage	An employee inflates purchase orders and splits the excess funds with a supplier
Sales Schemes	Manipulating sales transactions to inflate or distort reported revenue	A sales manager records fake sales at year-end to meet performance bonuses
Net Worth/Income Overstatements	Intentionally inflating assets, revenues, or profits to make financial performance appear stronger	A company records revenue from unshipped goods to boost quarterly earnings
Net Worth/Income Understatements	Intentionally reducing reported income or assets, often to lower taxes or create reserves for future periods	Management delays recording income until the next year to reduce current tax liabilities
Timing Differences	Manipulating the timing of revenue recognition or expense reporting to mislead users of financial statements	A company records next quarter's sales in the current period to appear more profitable
Fictitious Revenues	Recording revenue from non-existent sales or customers	An accountant creates fake customer accounts and invoices to inflate total sales
Concealed Liabilities and Expenses	Omitting or delaying the recording of legitimate liabilities or expenses to make financial performance look better	A business fails to record outstanding supplier bills, thereby reducing total reported expenses
Improper Asset Valuations	Misstating the value of assets to inflate or deflate their reported worth	A company overvalues obsolete inventory at full cost instead of writing it down
Improper Disclosures	Withholding or misrepresenting important information in financial statements could affect stakeholder decisions	Management fails to disclose a major pending lawsuit that could significantly affect profits
Understated Revenues	Deliberately recording less income than earned, often to defer profits or reduce taxes	A firm delays issuing invoices to clients until the next fiscal year to shift income
Overstated Liabilities and Expenses	Recording exaggerated or false expenses to understate profits or create reserves	A company records extra warranty expenses to reduce reported income and build future "cookie jar" reserves

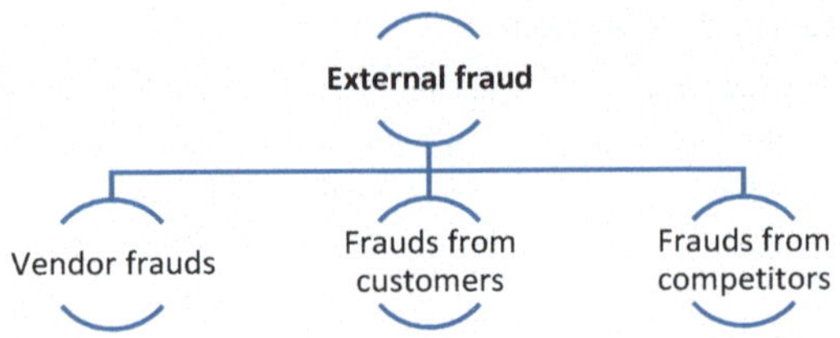

Fig. 3.3 External fraud tree. Source: Adopted from Occupational Fraud 2024: A Report to the Nations

Table 3.4 Vendor fraud schemes, definitions, and hypothetical examples

Vendor fraud scheme	Definition	Hypothetical example
Short Shipments	Occur when a vendor delivers fewer goods or lower-quality items than what was ordered or paid for, while invoicing the organization for the full amount	A supplier agrees to deliver 1000 units of office supplies but ships only 900, yet bills the company for all 1000 units. Because internal controls are weak, the discrepancy goes unnoticed
Balance Billing	Involves a vendor intentionally billing the organization for the full contract amount even after receiving partial payments or providing partial goods or services	A contractor receives a 50% advance payment for a project but later issues an invoice for the full contract value without deducting the initial payment. The overbilling remains undetected due to poor invoice verification
Fraudulent Cost-Plus Billing	Occurs when a vendor inflates the reported costs on a cost-plus contract, enabling them to earn a higher profit because payment is based on costs plus a markup	A construction vendor with a cost-plus contract reports inflated material costs and adds a 15% markup on the falsified amount, resulting in overpayment by the organization

3.3.2.2 Frauds from Customers

Customers can commit fraud against organisations through various methods. Examples include accounts receivable fraud (as previously mentioned) and returns fraud. In a returns fraud scheme, a customer might buy a product and then return a different, lower-quality item instead [17–19]. Similar to vendor fraud, most types of customer fraud exploit gaps or weaknesses in an organisation's internal control system. Table 3.5 provides definitions and hypothetical examples of each scheme.

3.3.2.3 Frauds from Competitors

Competitors may also engage in fraudulent activities against other organisations. Two common examples are sabotage and theft of proprietary information. There are countless ways a company might attempt to sabotage a competition. For instance, a competitor could damage another company's reputation by releasing low-quality counterfeit versions of its products. Theft of proprietary information is a form of corporate espionage, which can take many forms. Competitors might obtain confidential data or trade secrets through methods such as wiretapping, hacking, or bribery [14, 20–22]. Table 3.6 provides definitions and hypothetical examples of each scheme.

3.3.3 Individual Fraud

Most people have reported being victims of fraud or at least being prone to it [23]. Identity Theft and one-on-one fraud are the most common types of fraud perpetrated against individuals [5]. Identity theft is defined as "one individual fraudulently obtaining goods, funds, or services under someone else's name" [5]. Examples of identity theft include, but are not limited to, obtaining tax refunds using stolen identities, obtaining goods and services using stolen credit cards and bank accounts, and obtaining funds through stolen insurance claims. Similarly, one-to-one fraud

Table 3.5 Frauds from customers' schemes, definitions, and hypothetical examples

Customer fraud scheme	Definition	Hypothetical example
Accounts Receivable Fraud	Occurs when a customer manipulates or deceives the organization's credit or payment process to avoid paying what they owe or to obtain unauthorized benefits	A customer alters an invoice to show a smaller balance due and pays the reduced amount, cheating the company out of the full payment
Returns Fraud	Involves the return of stolen or substituted merchandise for a refund, credit, or exchange, often using falsified receipts or deceitful tactics	A customer purchases a new electronic device, replaces it with an old or defective unit, and then returns it, claiming it was unused or faulty

Table 3.6 Frauds from competitors' schemes, definitions, and hypothetical examples

Competitor fraud scheme	Definition	Hypothetical example
Sabotage	Sabotage occurs when a competing organization deliberately takes actions intended to damage another company's operations, products, or reputation to gain a competitive advantage. This can include spreading false information, interfering with supply chains, or introducing counterfeit products	A competing company produces and distributes counterfeit versions of another firm's popular product, causing customers to associate the poor-quality items with the original brand and damaging its market reputation
Theft of Proprietary Information	Theft of proprietary information, also known as corporate espionage, involves illegally obtaining confidential business data, trade secrets, or strategic plans from a competitor. This can be achieved through hacking, wiretapping, bribery, or insider infiltration	A competing firm hacks into another company's server to steal product design files and uses the stolen information to launch a similar product ahead of the original company's release

involves directly targeting an individual by building trust or creating a personal connection to deceive them for financial or personal gain. Examples include personal investment scams, catfishing, and door-to-door scams in which fraudsters pose as service providers or offer assistance. These scams rely heavily on emotional manipulation, personal persuasion, and the cultivation of the victim's confidence before exploiting it [24–26].

3.4 Fraud Impact

Fraud is deemed a major problem in this era, with no one immune. The Occupational Fraud: A Report to the Nations presents a comprehensive analysis of occupational fraud based on a global study encompassing 1921 cases across 138 countries and territories, totaling losses exceeding $3.1 billion.[2] According to the report, organizations worldwide are estimated to lose approximately 5% of their annual revenue to fraud, with the average loss per case totaling $1.7 million and the median loss estimated at $145,000. Among the various types of fraudulent schemes identified, asset misappropriation was the most prevalent, accounting for 89% of cases, though it incurred comparatively lower losses, with a median of $120,000. Conversely, financial statement fraud was the least common, accounting for only 5% of cases, but resulted in the highest median loss of $766,000. Corruption emerged as another significant form of occupational fraud, present in 48% of all reported cases. The typical fraudulent activity was found to persist for approximately 12 months before detection, suggesting delays in organizational response and oversight.

The report further highlights that the majority of frauds were detected through tips, accounting for 43% of cases, more than three times the next most common detection method. Email and web-based reporting mechanisms have surpassed traditional telephone hotlines as the dominant means of reporting, with more than half of tips originating from employees, and nearly one-third from vendors and customers. Regarding outcomes, 57% of fraud cases were referred to law enforcement, and 72% of those referrals resulted in convictions. Among cases not referred, 68% of perpetrators were dismissed from their positions. In comparison, organizations that opted not to involve authorities often cited internal discipline (49%) or concerns about reputational damage (34%) as the main reasons for their decision.

The findings also reveal significant variations in losses across organizational types and industries. Nonprofit organizations experienced the lowest median losses at $76,000, compared to $150,000 for government, public, and private entities. By industry, mining reported the highest median losses at $550,000, followed by wholesale trade ($361,000), manufacturing ($267,000), construction ($250,000), and real estate/government ($200,000). Importantly, 82% of victim organizations implemented improvements to their anti-fraud controls after experiencing an

[2] https://www.acfe.com/-/media/files/ACFE/PDFs/RTTN/2024/Infographics/Key-Findings.pdf

incident, and 27% of these modifications were expected to be highly effective in preventing future occurrences. The absence of adequate internal controls (32%) and the overriding of existing controls (19%) were identified as the leading enablers of fraud, with evidence indicating that robust anti-fraud mechanisms correlate with lower financial losses and faster detection.

Regarding perpetrators, the study found that fraud committed by owners or executives resulted in losses more than seven times higher than those committed by lower-level employees, with median losses of $459,000 and $60,000, respectively. More than half of all cases originated from five departments: operations (14%), accounting (12%), sales (12%), customer service (9%), and executive management (9%). Additionally, collusion among multiple perpetrators significantly increased losses, with schemes involving three or more individuals resulting in median losses exceeding those in single-offender cases by a factor of 4. The report also established a positive relationship between tenure and fraud magnitude: employees with less than 1 year of service caused a median loss of $50,000. In contrast, those with over 10 years of service caused losses averaging $250,000. Notably, 84% of fraudsters exhibited at least one behavioral red flag, underscoring the importance of employee monitoring and behavioral assessment in fraud prevention.

The report underscores the pervasive and costly nature of occupational fraud across industries and organizational structures. They highlight the critical role of internal control systems, employee awareness, and structured reporting mechanisms in mitigating fraud risk. The study concludes that organizations with proactive fraud detection measures and strong governance frameworks not only experience lower financial losses but also achieve quicker identification and resolution of fraudulent activities.

3.5 Investigation Tools

Forensic accountants utilise two approaches when conducting investigations (i.e., behavioural indicators approach and financial data approach) [27]. These approaches are fundamentally different; however, both complement each other. The use of the behavioural indicator approach is based on the idea that all fraudsters are driven by specific factors to commit fraud [28]. Section 3.5.1. illustrates the behavioural aspects of fraudsters and how forensic accountants can investigate them. Furthermore, users of financial data in fraud investigations employ a range of statistical analysis techniques to detect indicators of fraud within a financial dataset. Section 3.5.2. highlights the statistical analysis techniques available to forensic accountants in fraud investigation.

3.5.1 Behavioral Indicators Approach to Investigate Fraud

In the fraud investigations literature, authors have proposed various psychological and behavioural motivations for committing fraud. The exploration of the circumstances and motivations behind fraud began in the late 1940s when psychologist Donald Cressey conducted his PhD thesis to understand why innocent people become fraudsters [3, 29, 30]. Cressey visited jails to interview prisoners serving time for financial crimes. He aimed to identify common patterns among them to answer the question of why innocent individuals turn to fraud. According to Cressey's study, three main factors strongly motivate fraudulent behaviour. These are opportunity, rationalisation, and pressure, later known as the fraud triangle theory [31–34]. Figure 3.4 illustrates the fraud triangle.

The first factor, opportunity, relates to a situation or control weakness that permits fraud to happen with a low risk of detection. The second factor, which is the pressure factor, concerns a personal or financial need that motivates someone to commit fraud. The third factor, rationalisation, concerns the mental justification that leads the fraudster to believe their actions are acceptable [35, 36].

Further researchers have expanded the fraud triangle theory by introducing new factors. For example, Wolfe and Hermanson [37] presented the fraud diamond model, which extends the fraud triangle theory by adding a fourth factor: the capability factor (see Fig. 3.5). Capability refers to the perpetrator's unique ability to commit fraud. Furthermore, [4] emphasises integrity as a determinant of fraud behaviour. Albrecht claims that an individual with strong personal integrity would not easily rationalise unethical behaviour.

Later on, Vousinas [38] developed fraud theories by adding two factors, as shown in Figs. 3.6 and 3.7. These factors are ego and collusion. Ego refers to a situation in which a fraudster is confident that they will not be detected while committing fraud. Collusion refers to a deceitful agreement or compact between two or more persons, whereby one party brings an action against the other for a malicious purpose.

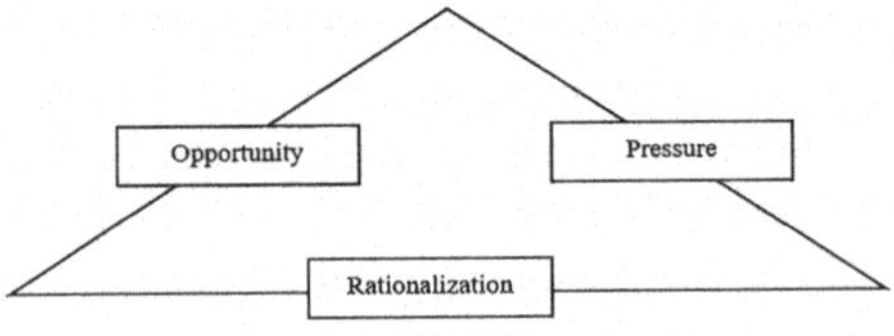

Fig. 3.4 Fraud triangle theory

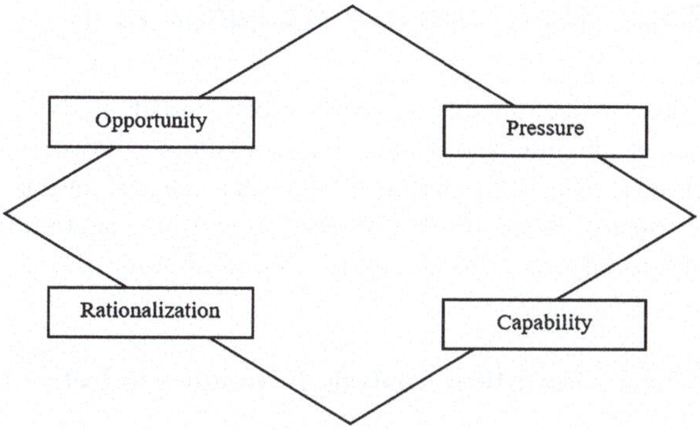

Fig. 3.5 Fraud diamond model. Source: Wolfe and Hermanson [37]

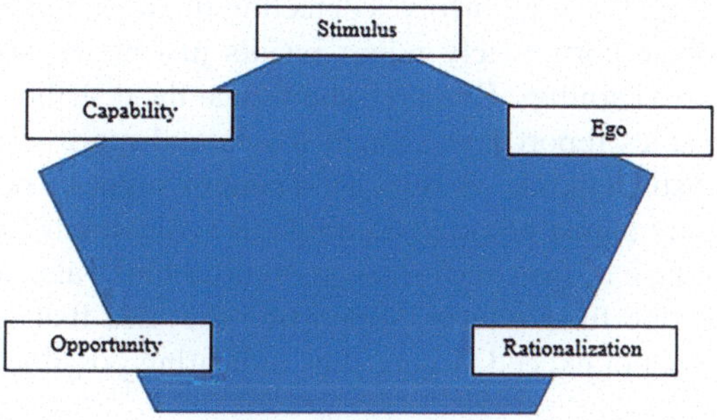

Fig. 3.6 Fraud pentagon model. Source: Vousinas [38]

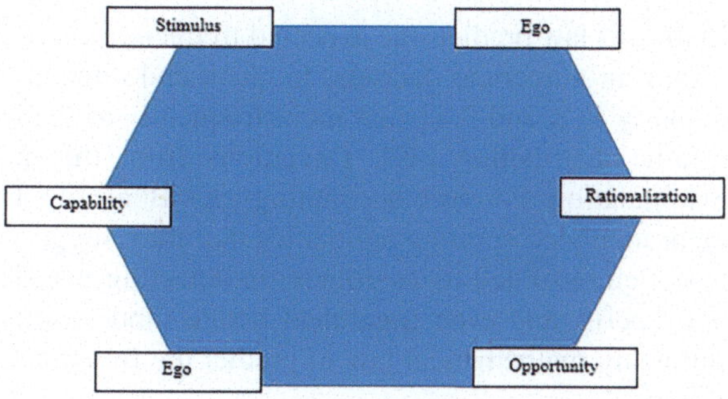

Fig. 3.7 Fraud hexagon model. Source: Vousinas [38]

3.5.2 Prevention and Mitigation Tools

Forensic accountants employ various statistical and accounting-based techniques to detect and uncover fraud. The statistical analysis techniques focus on statistical abnormalities and include tools such as target beating, Benford's law, and anomalies in post-decimal digits. At the same time, accounting-based techniques include abnormal accruals and audit-based predictors [27].

3.5.2.1 Statistical Analysis Techniques to Detect Fraud

3.5.2.1.1 Target Beating

Target beating involves detecting financial misconduct by examining whether firms disproportionately report results just above key performance thresholds, such as zero earnings. Research shows that the distribution of firm earnings is uneven: companies report fewer small losses and more small gains than expected, creating a distinct "kink" at zero. This pattern suggests deliberate manipulation, as managers may adjust reported earnings to avoid small losses and project a more favourable image of firm performance. Similar kinks also appear in analyst forecast errors and hedge fund returns, supporting the idea that some firms alter reported figures to meet or exceed targets, thus indicating possible misreporting [27].

3.5.2.1.2 Benford's Law

Benford's law predicts the expected frequency distribution of first digits in naturally occurring numerical datasets. In clean and unmanipulated data, lower digits, particularly 1, 2, and 3, appear more frequently as the leading digit, following a logarithmic distribution [39]. Deviations from this pattern can indicate errors or manipulation. Forensic accounting uses Benford's law to examine financial statement numbers, spotting anomalies that may suggest financial misconduct. Studies have demonstrated its usefulness in detecting inaccurate earnings, misstated internal reports, and even fraudulent hedge fund returns [40]. Benford suggested the following mathematical law to predict the frequencies of the first digits in a given dataset.

$$P(d) = \log_{10}(1 + 1/d), \text{where } d = 1, 2, \ldots, 9.$$

According to Benford's law, each number has an expected percentage to exist in the first digit in a given large dataset. Table 3.7 shows the expected percentage for each number.

3.5.2.1.3 Abnormalities in Post-Decimal Digits

Abnormalities in post-decimal digits examine the digits beyond the decimal point in financial metrics such as earnings per share (EPS). Because EPS is rounded to the nearest cent, firms have an incentive to report post-decimal digits of five or higher to round earnings upward. Research finds that the digits immediately above five occur more frequently than expected, suggesting potential rounding manipulation. A specific pattern known as *Quadrophobia* refers to the unusual underrepresentation of the digit "4" in the first post-decimal place. Firms exhibiting Quadrophobia are more likely to restate financials, face regulatory enforcement, or be sued for securities fraud, making it a strong predictor of potential misconduct [41–43].

3.5.2.2 Accounting-Based Techniques to Detect Fraud

3.5.2.2.1 Abnormal Accruals

Abnormal accruals are accounting indicators that suggest potential earnings manipulation. Under accrual accounting, firms record revenues and expenses when earned or incurred, not necessarily when cash is received or paid. While some accrual activity is normal, unusually high or abnormal accruals may indicate that firms are artificially enhancing their performance by overstating receivables or understating expenses. Researchers estimate expected accrual levels based on economic fundamentals and compare them with reported accruals to identify discrepancies [43].

3.5.2.2.2 Audit-Based Predictors

Audit-based predictors examine auditors' and audit processes' characteristics to identify firms at higher risk of financial reporting misconduct. Auditors differ in quality, and research shows that clients of larger, more reputable audit firms are less likely to misreport financial results [43, 44]. Differences also exist across individual

Table 3.7 Benford's distribution

Digit	Expected benford (%)
1	30.1
2	17.6
3	12.5
4	9.7
5	7.9
6	6.7
7	5.8
8	5.1
9	4.6

audit offices and even among engagement partners, with some consistently associated with higher or lower audit quality. Firms audited by lower-quality auditors or by offices and partners with weaker track records tend to exhibit higher levels of misreporting and restatements. As regulatory disclosures about auditors expand, these audit-based indicators become increasingly powerful predictors of misconduct [2, 7, 45–47].

3.6 Conclusion

Fraud investigation sits at the intersection of accounting, law, and investigative science, requiring practitioners to combine analytical accuracy with professional scepticism. This chapter has emphasised that effective fraud detection and investigation extend beyond routine financial reviews. The success of a fraud investigation relies on the investigator's capacity to stay objective, maintain the integrity of evidence, and communicate findings in a clear, convincing, and legally robust manner. By mastering the principles outlined in this chapter, forensic accountants strengthen their ability to safeguard organisations, support legal processes, and maintain the wider public trust in financial reporting and corporate governance.

References

1. Kaur, B., K. Sood, and S. Grima, *A systematic review on forensic accounting and its contribution towards fraud detection and prevention.* Journal of Financial Regulation and Compliance, 2023. **31**(1): p. 60–95.
2. Mandal, A., *Preventing financial statement fraud in the corporate sector: insights from auditors.* Journal of Financial Reporting and Accounting, 2023.
3. Wardani, D.K. and A.T. Putri. *The fraud triangle of accounting students' academic cheating.* in *Proceeding of International Conference on Accounting and Finance.* 2023.
4. Albrecht, W.S., et al., *Fraud examination.* 2006: Thomson South-Western New York, NY.
5. Crain, M.A., et al., *Essentials of forensic accounting.* 2019: John Wiley & Sons.
6. Clavería Navarrete, A. and A. Carrasco Gallego, *Forensic accounting tools for fraud deterrence: a qualitative approach.* Journal of Financial Crime, 2023. **30**(3): p. 840–854.
7. Hassan, S.W.U., et al., *The perception of accountants/auditors on the role of corporate governance and information technology in fraud detection and prevention.* Journal of Financial Reporting and Accounting, 2023.
8. Jain, A.K., *Corruption: A review.* Journal of economic surveys, 2001. **15**(1): p. 71–121.
9. Lehmann, C.M., *Asset misappropriation schemes: Short cases for Use in the classroom.* Journal of Forensic & Investigative Accounting, 2015. **7**(2): p. 340–362.
10. Azad, A., M. Salehi, and M. Lari Dashtbayaz, *An empirical study on the materiality calculation at financial statements level.* Journal of Public Affairs, 2022. **22**(4): p. e2608.
11. Ilter, C., *Misrepresentation of financial statements: An accounting fraud case from Turkey.* Journal of Financial Crime, 2014.
12. Gabrielli, G. and A. Medioli, *An overview of instruments and tools to detect fraudulent financial statements.* Universal Journal of Accounting and Finance, 2019. **7**(3): p. 76–82.

13. Akinbowale, O.E., H.E. Klingelhöfer, and M.F. Zerihun, *An innovative approach in combating economic crime using forensic accounting techniques.* Journal of Financial Crime, 2020. **27**(4): p. 1253–1271.
14. Ozili, P.K., *Advances and issues in fraud research: a commentary.* Journal of Financial Crime, 2020. **27**(1): p. 92–103.
15. Yang, C.-H. and K.-C. Lee, *Developing a strategy map for forensic accounting with fraud risk management: An integrated balanced scorecard-based decision model.* Evaluation and program planning, 2020. **80**: p. 101780.
16. Alzoubi, A.B., *Maximizing internal control effectiveness: the synergy between forensic accounting and corporate governance.* Journal of Financial Reporting and Accounting, 2023.
17. Salehi, M. and F. Norouzi, *The effect of corporate lobbying on fraud and money laundering.* Journal of Money Laundering Control, 2022.
18. Yusuf, M. and K. Harefa. *Forensic Accounting and Compliance Audit to Reduce the Number of Financial Fraud in Local Government.* in *2nd International Conference of Strategic Issues on Economics, Business and, Education (ICoSIEBE 2021).* 2022. Atlantis Press.
19. Al Natour, A.R., et al., *The role of forensic accounting skills in fraud detection and the moderating effect of CAATTs application: evidence from Egypt.* Journal of Financial Reporting and Accounting, 2023.
20. Burzinji, Z., et al., *The effect of forensic accounting on fraud prevention, the moderating role internal control effectiveness.* International Journal of Economics, Commerce and Management, 2022. **10**(1): p. 213–230.
21. Afriyie, S.O., et al., *Forensic accounting: A novel paradigm and relevant knowledge in fraud detection and prevention.* International Journal of Public Administration, 2023. **46**(9): p. 615–624.
22. Akinbowale, O.E., H.E. Klingelhöfer, and M.F. Zerihun, *Application of forensic accounting techniques in the South African banking industry for the purpose of fraud risk mitigation.* Cogent Economics & Finance, 2023. **11**(1): p. 2153412.
23. Kadoya, Y., et al., *Who is next? A study on victims of financial fraud in Japan.* Frontiers in Psychology, 2021. **12**: p. 649565.
24. Anisykurlillah, I., et al., *Examining the role of sharia supervisory board attributes in reducing financial statement fraud by Islamic banks.* Banks and Bank Systems, 2020. **15**(3): p. 106–116.
25. Barnes, J., *Fraud Detection: Forensic Accounting Education and CFE Designation Impact on Auditor's Confidence Levels.* Journal of Accounting and Finance, 2020. **20**(4): p. 62–75.
26. Öztürk, M.S. and H. Usul, *Detection of Accounting Frauds Using the Rule-Based Expert Systems within the Scope of Forensic Accounting*, in *Contemporary Issues in Audit Management and Forensic Accounting*. 2020, Emerald Publishing Limited.
27. Honigsberg, C., *Forensic accounting.* Annual Review of Law and Social Science, 2020. **16**: p. 147–164.
28. Ozili, P.K., *Forensic accounting theory*, in *Uncertainty and Challenges in Contemporary Economic Behaviour*. 2020, Emerald Publishing Limited.
29. Cheliatsidou, A., et al., *The international fraud triangle.* Journal of Money Laundering Control, 2023. **26**(1): p. 106–132.
30. Alshurafat, H., et al., *Factors affecting accounting students' misuse of chatgpt: an application of the fraud triangle theory.* Journal of Financial Reporting and Accounting, 2024. **22**(2): p. 274–288.
31. Al Shbail, M.O., et al., *Factors affecting online cheating by accounting students: the relevance of social factors and the fraud triangle model factors.* Academy of Strategic Management Journal, 2021. **20**: p. 1–16.
32. Sánchez-Aguayo, M., L. Urquiza-Aguiar, and J. Estrada-Jiménez, *Fraud detection using the fraud triangle theory and data mining techniques: a literature review.* Computers, 2021. **10**(10): p. 121.
33. Tickner, P. and M. Button, *Deconstructing the origins of Cressey's Fraud Triangle.* Journal of Financial Crime, 2021. **28**(3): p. 722–731.

34. Alshurafat, H., et al., *Factors affecting accounting students' misuse of chatgpt: an application of the fraud triangle theory.* Journal of Financial Reporting and Accounting, 2023.
35. Said, J., et al., *Integrating ethical values into fraud triangle theory in assessing employee fraud: Evidence from the Malaysian banking industry.* Journal of International Studies, 2017. **10**(2).
36. Homer, E.M., *Testing the fraud triangle: a systematic review.* Journal of Financial Crime, 2020. **27**(1): p. 172–187.
37. Wolfe, D.T. and D.R. Hermanson, *The fraud diamond: Considering the four elements of fraud.* CPA Journal, 2004. **74**(12): p. 38–42.
38. Vousinas, G.L., *Advancing theory of fraud: the SCORE model.* Journal of Financial Crime, 2019. **26**(1): p. 372–381.
39. Patel, P.C., M.G. Tsionas, and M.J. Guedes, *Benford's law, small business financial reporting, and survival.* Managerial and Decision Economics, 2022. **43**(8): p. 3301–3315.
40. Kuruppu, N., *The application of Benford's Law in fraud detection: a systematic methodology.* International Business Research, 2019. **12**(10): p. 1–10.
41. Ahmad, S., M.S. Ibrahim, and R.M. Abdou, *Understanding the Role of Forensic Accountants in Due Diligence Within Organizations and Its Impact on Organizational Learning.* Sustainable Data Management: Navigating Big Data, Communication Technology, and Business Digital Leadership. Volume 1, 2025: p. 3–10.
42. Işik, B.K., *ETHICS IN FORENSIC ACCOUNTING: CHALLENGES, IMPACTS AND FUTURE DIRECTIONS.* Anadolu Üniversitesi İktisadi ve İdari Bilimler Fakültesi Dergisi, 2025. **26**(3): p. 316–337.
43. Ismail, S., R.M. Abdou, and M.S. Ibrahim, *Who is Better in Practicing Customer Due Diligence as an Anti-Money Laundering Tool for Financial Institutions: Can Internal Auditors Be Forensic Accountants? Evidence from MENA Region*, in *Sustainable Data Management: Navigating Big Data, Communication Technology, and Business Digital Leadership. Volume 1*. 2025, Springer. p. 11–23.
44. Alkhalaileh, R., et al., *The impact of external auditors with forensic accounting competencies on auditee firm performance.* Heliyon, 2024. **10**(11).
45. Haloush, H.A., H. Alshurafat, and A.A.A. Alhusban, *Auditors'civil liability towards clients under the jordanian law: legal and auditing perspectives.* Journal of Governance and Regulation/Volume, 2021. **10**(1).
46. Alshurafat, H., H. Al-Mawali, and M.O. Al Shbail, *The influence of technostress on the intention to use blockchain technology: the perspectives of Jordanian auditors.* Development and Learning in Organizations: An International Journal, 2022(ahead-of-print).
47. Shbail, A., et al. *The Impact of Job Stressors and Burnout on Internal Auditors' Satisfaction.* in *International Conference on Business and Technology*. 2023. Springer.

Chapter 4
The Role of Forensic Accounting in Detecting and Deterring Organised Financial Crimes

4.1 Introduction

In today's vexed business environment, there is a dramatic increase in financial crimes. Moreover, the types of financial crimes have become more sophisticated [1–7]. It has also been noticed that many organisations or groups of individuals are planning and committing organised financial crimes to gain illegal financial profits [8–15]. This chapter explains organised financial crime, including money laundering, high-profile corporate scandals, Ponzi and pyramid schemes, and identity theft. Moreover, this chapter illustrates the role that a forensic accountant plays in detecting and deterring each type of these organised financial crimes.

4.2 Money Laundering

4.2.1 The Definition and Impact of Money Laundering

Money laundering is the process of concealing the origins of illegally obtained funds by passing them through complex transactions, shell companies, or offshore accounts to make them appear legitimate. Generally speaking, money laundering is the process of making illegally obtained money appear legitimate [16]. High-profile money laundering cases attract significant public attention and media coverage. Many agencies, both national and international, try to measure organised crime and money laundering, often sharing their findings publicly [17]. For instance, the total revenue from organised crime was estimated at $800 billion in 2001, rising to $1.7 trillion by 2007. Although these estimates are old and have a wide margin of error, they highlight the significant scale of money laundering and organised crime today [18].

H. Alshurafat, *Forensic Accounting*, https://doi.org/10.1007/978-981-95-8613-4_4

4.2.2 Steps for Conducting Money Laundering

In money laundering, there are three main steps, which are placement, layering and integration as shown in Fig. 4.1. Each of these steps is associated with a primary task and a list of techniques for performing that task [19]. For example, in the placement step, the money launderer usually finds a way to deposit the funds in such a way to avoid suspicion. The techniques for the placement step are as follows.

- splitting large cash amounts into deposits under $10,000 to avoid government reporting;
- exchanging prepaid debit cards or negotiable instruments for goods or services;
- Using front businesses to mix illegal and legal funds
- acquiring or manipulating banks, especially in countries with weak oversight.

The second step involves layering, which means moving money, usually from one account to another, in a way that prevents tracing it back to the original deposit made in the placement step [20]. The techniques for the layering step are as follows.

- Informal value transfer systems (IVTSs): These facilitate the cross-border movement of money without formal institutions.
- Off-shore accounts: Some countries have banking laws that let money launderers move money without detection, often attracting tax evaders.
- Anonymous trusts in certain jurisdictions can conceal beneficiaries' identities, separating the money's source from its owner.
- Bearer stock certificates: In some countries, the true owners of companies can remain anonymous, making it difficult to trace funds to individuals.
- Walking accounts: Accounts with instructions to wire money elsewhere if investigated.
- Financial intermediaries: Launderers may use securities brokers or insurance companies to pass funds and disguise ownership.

In the third step, the integration step makes the illicit funds available to the money launderer [21, 22]. The techniques for the placement step are as follows.

- Converting money into prepaid or secured cards, often issued from foreign countries, for personal spending.
- Receiving large payments or loans from offshore companies controlled by the launderer.
- Disguising illegal funds as gambling winnings, which casinos can pay out via check or wire transfer.
- Selling worthless assets or using fake import/export sales to move large sums.

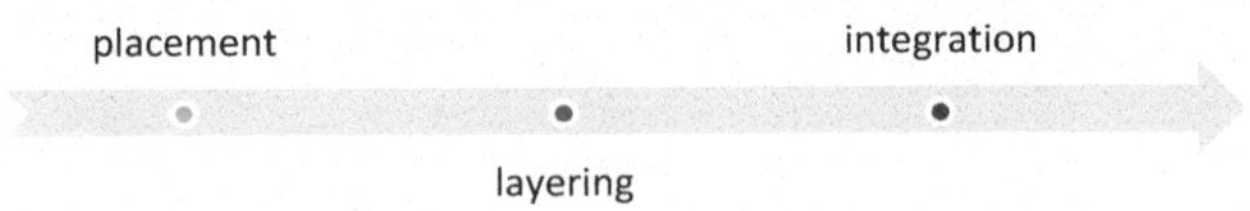

Fig. 4.1 Money laundering steps

- Concealing part of a sale (like real estate or yachts) by not reporting the full amount, with some funds paid in cash and unrecorded.
- Using dishonest brokers to create fake trading gains and paying them a fee to cover up the losses, leaving the launderer with usable funds.
- Injecting illicit cash into a business under the launderer's control, then withdrawing the money for personal use.

4.2.3 Scenarios and Cases for Money Laundering

4.2.3.1 Cash-Intensive Business (Restaurant or Car Wash)

Scenario:

A criminal earns large amounts of cash from illegal drug sales. To legitimise it, they buy a small restaurant.

How laundering happens:

- Illicit cash is mixed with real daily sales
- Fake receipts inflate revenue
- Money is deposited as "business income"

4.2.3.2 Real Estate Laundering

Scenario:

An individual purchases a luxury property using funds from corruption or fraud.

How laundering happens:

- Property bought through shell companies
- Sold later at a higher price
- Proceeds appear as legitimate investment gains

4.2.3.3 Trade-Based Money Laundering

Scenario:

A company over-invoices imported goods to move money across borders.

How laundering happens:

- Fake or inflated invoices
- Excess funds transferred to offshore accounts
- Money re-enters as "trade profits"

4.2.3.4 Online Gambling & Betting Platforms

Scenario:

Criminals use online casinos to clean stolen funds.

How laundering happens:

- Deposit illicit funds
- Place minimal bets
- Withdraw as "winnings"

4.2.3.5 Cryptocurrency Laundering

Scenario:

Hackers launder stolen money using cryptocurrencies.

How laundering happens:

- Convert cash to crypto
- Use mixers/tumblers to obscure trail
- Convert back to fiat currency

4.2.4 The Role of Forensic Accountants in Detecting Money Laundering

Money laundering supports criminal and terrorist activities, prompting more than 35 countries to cooperate through the Financial Action Task Force (FATF) [17, 23]. The FATF issues global anti-money laundering (AML) standards that many countries adopt, making it harder for launderers to find safe havens. These standards emphasise criminalising terrorist financing, freezing illicit assets, international cooperation, regulating informal value transfer systems, and monitoring non-compliant countries.

Forensic accountants play a key role in detecting and deterring money laundering within this framework. They analyse financial records, identify suspicious transaction patterns, investigate complex ownership structures, and assess compliance with AML regulations. By reviewing transaction reports, tracing illicit funds, and supporting regulatory enforcement, forensic accountants help financial institutions strengthen internal controls, meet reporting obligations, and reduce the risk of being used for money laundering [18, 24, 25].

4.3 High-Profile Corporate Scandals

4.3.1 The Definition and Impact of High-Profile Corporate Scandals

High-profile corporate scandals are large-scale frauds committed by organisations or senior management, such as falsifying financial statements, overstating revenues, or concealing liabilities (e.g., accounting scandals). Typically, these fraud costs are very high, reaching millions of dollars [26, 27]. Therefore, the impact of such organised crimes is devastating for the company itself and for society, as company stakeholders typically represent a broad range of individuals within society [28–30].

4.3.2 Examples of High-Profile Corporate Scandals

The following are examples of high-profile corporate scandals.

Financial Fraud & Accounting Scandals

- Enron (2001)—Massive accounting fraud using off-balance-sheet entities; led to bankruptcy and the collapse of Arthur Andersen.
- WorldCom (2002)—Inflated earnings by over $11 billion through improper accounting.
- Wirecard (2020)—1.9 billion euros in cash turned out not to exist; exposed major failures in European financial oversight.
- Parmalat (2003)—Italian dairy giant falsified accounts; 14 billion euros hole discovered.

Banking & Financial Misconduct

- Wells Fargo (2016)—Employees opened millions of fake customer accounts due to aggressive sales targets.
- Lehman Brothers (2008)—Used accounting manoeuvres ("Repo 105") to hide leverage before the financial crisis.
- HSBC (2012)—Allowed money laundering for drug cartels and sanctioned countries.

Automotive & Manufacturing

- Volkswagen "Dieselgate" (2015)—Installed software to cheat emissions tests; cost over $30 billion in fines and settlements.
- Takata (2014–2017)—Defective airbags caused deaths; led to the largest automotive recall in history.
- Boeing 737 MAX (2018–2019)—Design flaws and poor safety culture linked to two fatal crashes.

Tech & Data Privacy

- Facebook/Cambridge Analytica (2018)—Misuse of personal data from tens of millions of users for political profiling.
- Equifax (2017)—Data breach exposed personal information of ~147 million people due to poor security practices.
- Uber (2017)—Covered up a major data breach and faced revelations of systemic cultural problems.

Energy & Environmental

- BP Deepwater Horizon (2010)—Oil spill in the Gulf of Mexico; severe environmental damage and safety failures.
- PG&E (2018)—Faulty equipment linked to deadly California wildfires; the company later pleaded guilty to manslaughter.

Pharma & Healthcare

- Purdue Pharma (OxyContin)—Misleading marketing contributed to the opioid crisis.
- Theranos—Claimed revolutionary blood-testing technology that didn't work; executives convicted of fraud.
- Johnson & Johnson (opioids & talc)—Legal actions over misleading claims and product safety.

4.3.3 *Reasons Behind the High-Profile Corporate Scandals*

Researchers have identified the following as the most influential factors in the occurrence of high-profile corporate scandals.

- Weak corporate governance and board oversight
- Incentives that reward short-term gains over ethics
- Regulatory blind spots or failures
- Suppression of internal whistleblowers
- Culture that discourages transparency3

4.3.4 *The Role of Forensic Accounting Practitioners in Detecting Identity Theft*

Forensic accounting practitioners play a vital role in detecting high-profile corporate scandals by acting as financial investigators who identify, analyse, and prove fraud that is often concealed through complex accounting and weak governance [31, 32]. They examine financial statements for red flags, trace the flow of funds, reconstruct transactions, uncover falsified records, and quantify financial losses, going beyond routine audits to focus on intent, deception, and evidence [33–35]. Their work supports regulators, prosecutors, and courts by providing expert reports and testimony that help expose schemes such as financial statement fraud, corruption, money laundering, and Ponzi schemes, while also contributing to the prevention of future scandals through stronger internal controls and fraud risk management [36–39].

4.4 Ponzi and Pyramid Schemes

4.4.1 The Definition and Impact of Ponzi and Pyramid Schemes

Fraudulent investment operations where returns to earlier investors are paid using funds from new investors rather than legitimate profits [40]. Ponzi and pyramid schemes are types of financial fraud that promise unusually high or guaranteed returns, but do not generate real profits [41]. They survive only by using funds from new participants to repay earlier participants [42].

4.4.2 How the Ponzi Scheme Works?

A central organiser runs a Ponzi scheme. The Ponzi scheme works as follows.

- The organiser promises high, consistent returns.
- Early investors are paid using money from new investors, not real profits.
- It appears successful at first, which attracts more investors.
- The scheme collapses when new money stops coming in.

Key Features

- One main operator controls the money
- Fake or exaggerated investment results
- No real underlying business or profits

Famous Example

- Bernie Madoff, who ran the largest Ponzi scheme in history.

4.4.3 How Pyramid Scheme Work?

A pyramid scheme relies on recruitment rather than investment.

- Participants pay to join.
- They earn money mainly by recruiting others, not by selling real products or services.

- recruits pay those above them.
- Eventually, recruitment slows, and most people lose money.

4.5 Identity Theft

4.5.1 The Definition and Impact of Identity Fraud

Criminal networks create fake or blended identities to open accounts, obtain loans, or commit long-term financial fraud. Identity theft is when someone fraudulently obtains goods, funds, or services using another person's identity. Most cases are carried out by organised crime rings, often linked to other crimes, including tax-refund fraud, insurance fraud, mortgage fraud, bank fraud, and credit fraud. Victims can be individuals or businesses. Damages extend beyond financial loss and can seriously disrupt lives [16, 43].

Common methods include stealing Social Security numbers, addresses, or account details to access assets or credit. Thieves may also divert mail or alter identity data to avoid detection. Identity theft is illegal and punishable by imprisonment. Warning signs include unauthorised transactions, unknown accounts, or bills for things not purchased. Businesses are required to protect consumer data and notify victims [44–48]. Identity theft can be perpetrated through hacking, phishing, insider leaks, dumpster diving, social engineering, mailbox theft, street theft, or the misuse of public records and social media. There are over 15 million cases each year in the U.S. [43].

4.5.2 The Role of Forensic Accounting Practitioners in Detecting Identity Theft

Investigating identity theft involves tracing how data is stolen. Identity theft rings often include procurers, document forgers, sales managers, shoppers, and money launderers. Controlled delivery, in which law enforcement intercepts criminals during a transaction, is often used to apprehend perpetrators [49–57].

4.6 Conclusion

This chapter highlights that organised financial crimes, such as money laundering, high-profile corporate scandals, Ponzi and pyramid schemes, and identity theft, pose a serious and growing threat to modern economies due to their structured nature, sophistication, and significant financial and social consequences. This chapter demonstrates that these crimes are often facilitated by weak governance, complex financial systems, and technological advancements, allowing criminal networks to conceal illicit activities and infiltrate legitimate institutions. Within this context, forensic accounting emerges as a critical tool for both detection and deterrence, as forensic accountants apply specialised investigative, analytical, and legal skills to identify red flags, trace illicit funds, reconstruct fraudulent transactions, and support regulatory and judicial processes. By strengthening internal controls, enhancing transparency, and supporting law enforcement and regulators, forensic accounting plays a vital role in mitigating the impact of organised financial crime and promoting integrity, accountability, and trust in financial and corporate systems.

References

1. Hegazy, S., A. Sangster, and A. Kotb, *Mapping forensic accounting in the UK.* Journal of International Accounting, Auditing and Taxation, 2017. **28**: p. 43–56.
2. Kramer, B., M. Seda, and G. Bobashev, *Current opinions on forensic accounting education.* Accounting Research Journal, 2017. **30**(3): p. 249–264.
3. Said, J., et al., *Integrating ethical values into fraud triangle theory in assessing employee fraud: Evidence from the Malaysian banking industry.* Journal of International Studies, 2017. **10**(2).
4. Howieson, B., *What is the 'good'forensic accountant? A virtue ethics perspective.* Pacific Accounting Review, 2018. **30**(2): p. 155–167.
5. Rezaee, Z., J. Wang, and B. Lam, *Toward the integration of big data into forensic accounting education.* Journal of Forensic and Investigative Accounting, 2018. **10**(1): p. 87–99.
6. Alshurafat, H., et al. *The Domain of Forensic Accounting Services: Evidence from Australia.* in *19th Asian Academic Accounting Association (FourA) Annual Conference*. 2019.
7. Bunn, E., J. Ethridge, and K. Crow, *Fraud in small businesses: A preliminary study.* Journal of Accounting and Finance, 2019. **19**(3): p. 24–32.
8. Gabrielli, G. and A. Medioli, *An overview of instruments and tools to detect fraudulent financial statements.* Universal Journal of Accounting and Finance, 2019. **7**(3): p. 76–82.
9. Rezaee, Z. and J. Wang, *Relevance of big data to forensic accounting practice and education.* Managerial Auditing Journal, 2019. **34**(3): p. 268–288.
10. Seda, M.A., B. Peterson Kramer, and D.L. Crumbley, *An examination of computer forensics and related certifications in the accounting curriculum.* Journal of Digital Forensics, Security and Law, 2019. **14**(1): p. 4.
11. Taminiau, Y., S. Heusinkveld, and L. Cramer, *Colonization contests: How both accounting and law firms gain legitimacy in the market for forensic accounting.* Journal of Professions and Organization, 2019. **6**(1): p. 49–71.
12. Akinbowale, O.E., H.E. Klingelhöfer, and M.F. Zerihun, *An innovative approach in combating economic crime using forensic accounting techniques.* Journal of Financial Crime, 2020. **27** (4): p. 1253–1271.
13. Alhusban, A.A.A., et al., *The regulatory structure and governance of forensic accountancy in the emerging market: challenges and opportunities.* Journal of Governance and Regulation/ Volume, 2020. **9**(4): p. 149–161.
14. Alshurafat, H., et al., *Perceptions of the usefulness of various teaching methods in forensic accounting education.* Accounting Education, 2020. **29**(2): p. 177–204.
15. Anisykurlillah, I., et al., *Examining the role of sharia supervisory board attributes in reducing financial statement fraud by Islamic banks.* Banks and Bank Systems, 2020. **15**(3): p. 106–116.
16. Crain, M.A., et al., *Essentials of forensic accounting*. 2019: John Wiley & Sons.
17. Walker, J., *How big is global money laundering?* Journal of Money Laundering Control, 1999. **3**(1): p. 25–37.

18. Schneider, F. and U. Windischbauer, *Money laundering: some facts.* European Journal of Law and Economics, 2008. **26**(3): p. 387–404.
19. Ismail, S., R.M. Abdou, and M.S. Ibrahim, *Who is Better in Practicing Customer Due Diligence as an Anti-Money Laundering Tool for Financial Institutions: Can Internal Auditors Be Forensic Accountants? Evidence from MENA Region*, in *Sustainable Data Management: Navigating Big Data, Communication Technology, and Business Digital Leadership. Volume 1*. 2025, Springer. p. 11–23.
20. Chitimira, H. and S. Munedzi, *An evaluation of customer due diligence and related anti-money laundering measures in the United Kingdom.* Journal of Money Laundering Control, 2023. **26**(7): p. 127–137.
21. Salehi, M. and F. Norouzi, *The effect of corporate lobbying on fraud and money laundering.* Journal of Money Laundering Control, 2022.
22. Cheliatsidou, A., et al., *The international fraud triangle.* Journal of Money Laundering Control, 2023. **26**(1): p. 106–132.
23. Salehi, M., et al., *The effect of social and intellectual capital on fraud and money laundering in Iraq.* Journal of Money Laundering Control, 2022.
24. Molla Imeny, V., et al., *Perception versus reality: Iranian banks and international anti-money laundering expectations.* Journal of Money Laundering Control, 2021. **24**(1): p. 63–76.
25. Mousavi, M., et al., *The effect of corporate governance structure on fraud and money laundering.* Risks, 2022. **10**(9): p. 176.
26. Van Akkeren, J.K. and J.-A. Tarr, *The application of experiential learning for forensic accounting students: the Mock trial.* Accounting Education, 2021: p. 1–28.
27. Van Veldhoven, Z. and J. Vanthienen, *Digital transformation as an interaction-driven perspective between business, society, and technology.* Electronic Markets, 2022. **32**(2): p. 629–644.
28. Van Akkeren, J. and J.-A. Tarr, *Regulation, compliance and the Australian forensic accounting profession.* Journal of Forensic and Investigative Accounting, 2014. **6**(3): p. 1–26.
29. Tarr, J.-A., J. Van Akkeren, and S. Buckby, *Forensic accounting: Professional regulation of a multi-disciplinary field.* Australian Business Law Review, 2016. **44**(3): p. 204–215.
30. Van Akkeren, J. and S. Buckby, *Perceptions on the causes of individual and fraudulent co-offending: Views of forensic accountants.* Journal of Business Ethics, 2017. **146**(2): p. 383–404.
31. Kaur, B., K. Sood, and S. Grima, *A systematic review on forensic accounting and its contribution towards fraud detection and prevention.* Journal of Financial Regulation and Compliance, 2023. **31**(1): p. 60–95.
32. Alzahrane, M.A., *Insights from forensic accounting educators and practitioners within the KSA context regarding the optimal forensic accounting skills set: an implication on the socio-economic development.* Journal of Business and Socio-economic Development, 2024. **4**(1): p. 66–80.
33. Alzoubi, A.B., *Maximizing internal control effectiveness: the synergy between forensic accounting and corporate governance.* Journal of Financial Reporting and Accounting, 2023.
34. Clavería Navarrete, A. and A. Carrasco Gallego, *Forensic accounting tools for fraud deterrence: a qualitative approach.* Journal of Financial Crime, 2023. **30**(3): p. 840–854.
35. Street, D. and J. Wilck, *'Let's Have a Chat': Principles for the Effective Application of ChatGPT and Large Language Models in the Practice of Forensic Accounting.* Journal of Forensic and Investigative Accounting, July to December, 2023.
36. Al Natour, A.R., et al., *The role of forensic accounting skills in fraud detection and the moderating effect of CAATTs application: evidence from Egypt.* Journal of Financial Reporting and Accounting, 2023.
37. Al Shbeil, S., et al. *What Do We Know About Forensic Accounting? A Literature Review.* in *European, Asian, Middle Eastern, North African Conference on Management & Information Systems*. 2023. Springer.
38. Alshurafat, H., et al. *Forensic Accounting Education Within the Australian Universities.* in *International Conference on Business and Technology*. 2023. Springer.

39. Alshurafat, H., H.A. Haloush, and A.B.M. Alzoubi, *Forensic accounting from an Islamic perspective: a conceptual framework from the Jordanian context*, in *Islamic Accounting and Finance: A Handbook*. 2023, World Scientific. p. 173–193.
40. Hidajat, T., et al., *Why are people trapped in Ponzi and pyramid schemes?* Journal of Financial Crime, 2021. **28**(1): p. 187–203.
41. Nolasco, C.A.R., M.S. Vaughn, and R.V. Del Carmen, *Revisiting the choice model of Ponzi and Pyramid schemes: Analysis of case law.* Crime, law and social change, 2013. **60**(4): p. 375–400.
42. Hock, B. and M. Button, *Why do people join pyramid schemes?* Journal of Financial Crime, 2023. **30**(5): p. 1130–1139.
43. Archer, N., *Consumer identity theft prevention and identity fraud detection behaviours.* Journal of Financial Crime, 2011. **19**(1): p. 20–36.
44. Öztürk, M.S. and H. Usul, *Detection of accounting frauds using the rule-based expert systems within the scope of forensic accounting*, in *Contemporary issues in audit management and forensic accounting*. 2020, Emerald Publishing Limited.
45. Rehman, A. and F. Hashim, *Can forensic accounting impact sustainable corporate governance?* Corporate Governance: The International Journal of Business in Society, 2020.
46. Sahdan, M.H., C.J. Cowton, and J.E. Drake, *Forensic accounting services in English local government and the counter-fraud agenda.* Public Money & Management, 2020. **40**(5): p. 380–389.
47. Al Shbail, M.O., et al., *Dataset of Factors affecting online cheating by accounting students: The relevance of social factors and the fraud triangle model factors.* Data in Brief, 2021: p. 107732.
48. Al Shbail, M.O., et al., *Factors affecting online cheating by accounting students: the relevance of social factors and the fraud triangle model factors.* Academy of Strategic Management Journal, 2021. **20**: p. 1–16.
49. Alshurafat, H., *Forensic accounting as a profession in Australia? A sociological perspective.* Meditari Accountancy Research, 2021.
50. Ghofur, R.A. and A. Santika. *The Influence of Sharia Complaince Against Fraud on The Sharia Banks in Indonesia.* in *Annual Conference of Ihtifaz: Islamic Economics, Finance, and Banking*. 2021.
51. Wahyuni-TD, I.S., H. Haron, and Y. Fernando, *The effects of good governance and fraud prevention on performance of the zakat institutions in Indonesia: a Sharīʿah forensic accounting perspective.* International Journal of Islamic and Middle Eastern Finance and Management, 2021. **14**(4): p. 692–712.
52. Afriyie, S.O., et al., *Forensic accounting: a novel paradigm and relevant knowledge in fraud detection and prevention.* International Journal of Public Administration, 2022: p. 1–10.
53. Burzinji, Z., et al., *The effect of forensic accounting on fraud prevention, the moderating role internal control effectiveness.* International Journal of Economics, Commerce and Management, 2022. **10**(1): p. 213–230.
54. Ebaid, I.E.-S., *An exploration of accounting students' attitudes toward integrating forensic accounting in accounting education.* International Journal of Law and Management, 2022(ahead-of-print).
55. Ismail, S., et al., *A Review on Forensic Accounting Profession and Education: Global Context.* 2022.
56. Yusuf, M. and K. Harefa. *Forensic Accounting and Compliance Audit to Reduce the Number of Financial Fraud in Local Government.* in *2nd International Conference of Strategic Issues on Economics, Business and, Education (ICoSIEBE 2021)*. 2022. Atlantis Press.
57. Afriyie, S.O., et al., *Forensic accounting: A novel paradigm and relevant knowledge in fraud detection and prevention.* International Journal of Public Administration, 2023. **46**(9): p. 615–624.

Chapter 5
The Role of Forensic Accountants in Litigation Support

5.1 Introduction

As business transactions become more complex and global and local markets expand, incidents of financial manipulation, fraud, and corruption have increased [1–3]. Consequently, there is a rising demand for specialised professionals who can analyse financial data within a legal framework. Forensic accountants play a crucial role in litigation support, arbitration, and dispute resolution, where they assist in assessing financial claims, investigating irregularities, and clarifying complex financial information for judicial authorities [4–7].

Many financial disputes require highly qualified experts with strong academic backgrounds and practical experience in accounting, law, and management [8–12]. In this context, the forensic accountant functions as an expert witness whose opinions are based on objective financial analysis and adherence to legal standards [8]. Their work improves the efficiency and accuracy of judicial decision-making [4, 13, 14].

The origins of forensic accounting date back to the early twentieth century. The first recognised use of the term forensic accounting is attributed to Maurice Peloubet in 1946, marking the formal emergence of this specialised field [14]. Forensic accounting developed in response to the increasing need for accounting practices that support justice and legal proceedings [15–17].

Forensic accounting plays a vital role in today's economy, especially in tackling financial crimes, fraud, and complex commercial disputes [5, 18–20]. It is an interdisciplinary field that combines accounting, auditing, and legal expertise to support judicial institutions [21]. Through this combination, forensic accounting helps clarify financial facts and present reliable evidence to courts and regulatory authorities [18].

This study aims to enhance the understanding of the forensic accounting role in the litigation support domain by analysing its concept, objectives, and professional

H. Alshurafat, *Forensic Accounting*, https://doi.org/10.1007/978-981-95-8613-4_5

role within the judicial system. It emphasises the importance of forensic accountants' duties, qualifications, and ethical responsibilities, as well as the practical procedures employed in forensic accounting engagements. Moreover, this study highlights the essential role of forensic accounting in supporting justice and resolving financial disputes with professionalism and credibility.

5.2 The Role of Forensic Accountants Within the Courts

The role of forensic accounting within the court can vary depending on the jurisdictional context in which a forensic accountant works. Generally speaking, a forensic accounting practitioner primarily provides expert witness and consulting services, as shown in Fig. 5.1.

5.2.1 Expert Witness

Among litigation support services, expert witness services are the most commonly offered by forensic accounting firms [13, 22]. An expert witness service for a forensic accountant is a professional service where a forensic accountant is engaged to analyse financial evidence and provide independent expert opinions in legal disputes. In court, expert witnesses may provide opinions on matters before the court. Fact witnesses are experts who testify based on what they perceive through their senses. Therefore, Judges rely on expert and fact witnesses when making decisions. Expert witnesses are not permitted to advocate for any party in a legal case. Instead, their role is solely to help the judges by providing scientific, technical, or specialised knowledge [23].

Durtschi and Rufus [24] provided a teaching note illustrating the role of a forensic accountant as an expert witness who testifies in court and helps the judge determine whether an arson or an accident occurred. Moreover, Cooper and Kawada [18] allowed students to apply critical thinking and problem-solving to address a supplier-customer commercial damages litigation case. They analyse a fact pattern, review financial data and interviews, and answer questions on forensic accounting and professional practice. Finally, they prepare a commercial damages report to

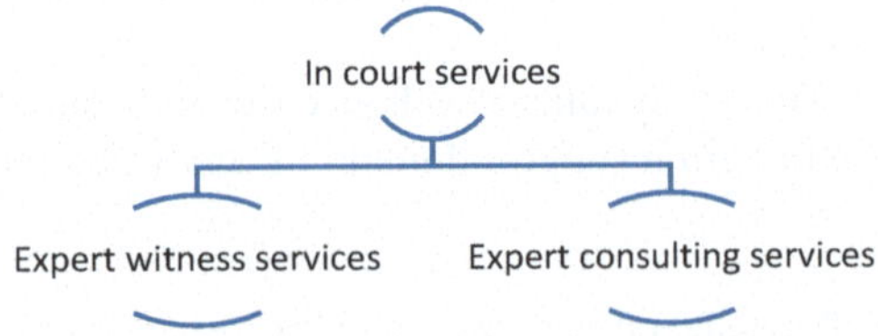

Fig. 5.1 Forensic accounting services within the court

communicate their analysis. The following are common tasks usually done by an expert witness.

- Assisting attorneys with case strategy from a financial perspective
- Reviewing opposing expert reports
- Preparing exhibits, schedules, and financial models
- Writing formal expert witness reports that explain findings clearly for judges, juries, and arbitrators
- Supporting opinions with calculations, documentation, and professional standards
- Providing oral testimony in depositions, hearings, or trials
- Explaining complex financial matters in plain language
- Withstanding cross-examination while maintaining independence and credibility

5.2.2 *Expert Consulting*

Expert consulting work is very similar to expert witness work. The primary distinction between an expert consultant and an expert witness lies in their roles during litigation. An expert consultant is typically engaged to provide specialised knowledge and guidance to attorneys as they build their case. Unlike an expert witness, an expert consultant does not testify in court and is generally not subject to discovery. Both expert consultants and expert witnesses may prepare detailed reports and provide professional opinions [1, 5]. However, while the materials generated by an expert consultant are usually intended for internal use, there remains a possibility that these reports could be introduced in court if circumstances change. Additionally, a forensic accountant initially retained as an expert consultant may later be designated as an expert witness if the case's needs evolve. In this situation, the professional would then provide testimony for the same client in the same legal matter, shifting from a behind-the-scenes advisory role to a public testimony role [6, 15, 16].

5.3 The Role of Forensic Accountants Outside the Courts (Financial Dispute Resolutions)

Most financial disputes are resolved outside court [14]. Therefore, resolving financial disputes is one of the most important forensic accounting services. These services are formally known as alternative dispute resolution services. Abdul-Baki [8] examines the forensic accountant's role in resolving disputes and promoting accountability among Nigerian government agents. Using a single case and mediation theory, it finds that PwC resolved the dispute, but government inaction limited accountability. The case demonstrates the value of forensic accounting in conflict resolution, its limitations, and the importance of professional integrity. Outside the court and within the domain of dispute resolution, forensic accounting practitioners typically provide three main services, as shown in Fig. 5.2.

5.3.1 Negotiation

Negotiation involves forensic accountants' direct participation in settlement discussions, where they perform a range of essential functions. These professionals provide financial analysis to assess various settlement options, model scenarios to forecast potential outcomes, evaluate risks and exposures associated with each option, and verify the accuracy of the parties' financial claims [20]. By providing these services, forensic accountants help ensure that settlement negotiations are grounded in reliable financial information and that the parties can make informed decisions through comprehensive analysis and risk assessment [7].

5.3.2 Mediation

Mediation involves the active participation of forensic accountants who assist parties in reaching a voluntary settlement by providing a comprehensive range of financial services. Their role includes quantifying economic damages, which is essential for understanding the potential financial implications of different settlement options. They also conduct detailed analyses of financial records and transactions to uncover relevant facts and ensure the accuracy of the financial information presented [8]. Additionally, forensic accountants are responsible for valuing businesses or assets involved in the dispute and for preparing neutral financial summaries that facilitate clear communication and understanding between the parties. By helping mediators achieve financial clarity, these professionals support the creation of an environment where informed and fair resolutions can be reached based on objective financial insights [14].

In the mediation process, a forensic accounting practitioner can play two roles:

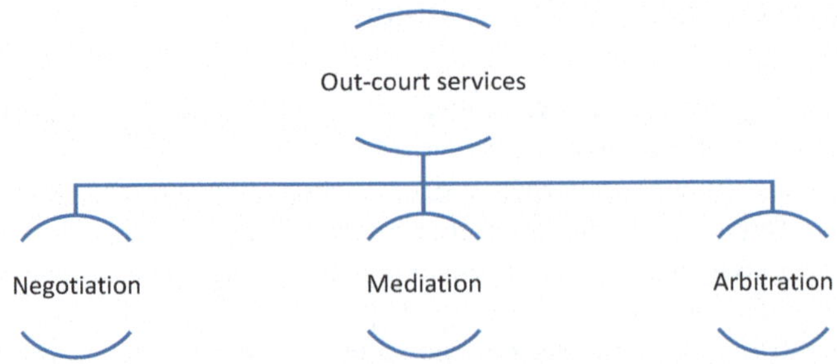

Fig. 5.2 Outside the court: Litigation support services through forensic accounting

1. Facilitative mediator adopts a nonjudgmental approach to help opposing parties understand each other's positions, communicate effectively, and find common ground.
2. Evaluative mediator: provides opinions and advice to both parties.

5.3.3 Arbitration

Arbitration is a less formal alternative to trial, with courts granted broad discretion under the law to set arbitration rules. These rules permit discovery, testimony, cross-examination, and the admission of evidence, though evidentiary standards are typically more relaxed than in court. Arbitration involves submitting disputes to a neutral third party. In binding arbitration, the neutral's decision is legally enforceable; in nonbinding arbitration, the outcome is advisory only. While parties may agree to arbitrate after a dispute arises, it is common for contracts to require arbitration for future disputes [8].

Arbitration may be administered or non-administered. Administered arbitration uses rules from organisations such as the American Arbitration Association, which also provides model agreements and helps with selecting arbitrators. In non-administered arbitration, the parties must agree on the process themselves, often each selecting an arbitrator, who then jointly chooses a third. The parties must also agree on the rules governing the arbitration, either by adopting the arbitrators' proposed rules or by negotiating their own [14].

5.3.4 Advantages and Disadvantages of Alternative Dispute Resolution

As demonstrated in Table 5.1, alternative dispute resolution entails both advantages and disadvantages.

5.4 Other Litigation Support Services

As discussed in Chap. 1, litigation support services are widespread and encompass more than just expert witnesses and consulting. The following are examples of what a forensic accounting practitioner could perform.

Table 5.1 Advantages and disadvantages of alternative dispute resolution

Advantages	Disadvantages
Cost-Effective: Usually more affordable than litigation because of reduced legal costs and quicker processes	Limited Right to Appeal: Arbitration decisions are typically final, with very limited avenues for appeal
Time-Saving: Disputes are resolved more quickly than lengthy court procedures	No Guaranteed Resolution: Mediation and negotiation may fail if the parties cannot reach an agreement
Confidentiality: Proceedings are private and protect sensitive personal or business information	Power Imbalance: Stronger parties may pressure weaker parties into unfair settlements
Flexibility: Parties can choose the process, timing, venue, and even the neutral third party (mediator/arbitrator)	Enforceability Issues: Some ADR outcomes (especially mediation) require court approval to be legally enforceable
Expert Decision-Makers: Arbitrators or mediators can be selected for their specialised expertise (e.g., finance, construction, accounting)	Costs Can Still Be High: Arbitration may be expensive due to arbitrator fees and administrative expenses
Preserves Relationships: Less adversarial than court proceedings, helping maintain business or personal relationships	Limited Discovery: Fewer opportunities to obtain evidence compared to court litigation
Reduced Formality: Procedures are less rigid than those under court rules, thereby facilitating participation	Lack of Legal Precedent: ADR decisions do not create binding legal precedents
Party Control: Parties have greater control over the outcome, particularly in mediation, where agreements are reached through mutual negotiation	Possible Bias: Concerns may arise if the neutral party is perceived as biased or repeatedly appointed by one side

- **Design compliance programs**

  The process of developing and implementing policies, procedures, and controls to ensure an organisation complies with laws, regulations, ethical standards, and internal policies, and to prevent, detect, and respond to violations.
- **Divorce & matrimonial matters**
  Legal proceedings relating to the dissolution of a marriage, including asset division, business valuation, income assessment, spousal support, child maintenance, and identification of hidden or undisclosed assets.
- **Shadow expert**
  A professional expert engaged to assist legal counsel behind the scenes by providing technical analysis, advice, and case strategy without testifying or being disclosed as an expert witness in court.

5.5 Qualifications for an Expert Witness

Qualifications can be demonstrated through knowledge, skills, experience, training, or education. Judges determine if an expert can testify in specific areas [14].

- The qualification process usually involves:
  - The retaining attorney presenting the expert's credentials
  - The opposing attorney challenging qualifications via cross-examination
- Key factors in qualifying an expert:
  - Prior testimony experience
  - Relevant education or training
  - Professional publications
  - Firsthand experience with the case

Practical experience can outweigh formal education; neither publications nor education alone are always necessary. In some cases, direct involvement in the matter is required for admissibility. Licences and professional designations often demonstrate expertise [25–29]. Judges consider all these factors to determine if an expert is suitable to testify in a particular case [17, 30].

5.6 Ethics, Skills, and Knowledge Required for Forensic Accountants in Litigation Support

For a forensic accounting practitioner providing litigation support services, it is essential to possess a comprehensive set of specialised ethical, technical, and professional skills and knowledge [31]. Table 5.2 displays these ethics and competencies and links them with the litigation support role of a forensic accountant.

5.7 Conclusion

This chapter has examined the critical role of forensic accountants in litigation support and financial dispute resolution within increasingly complex legal and business environments. As financial transactions become more sophisticated and the incidence of fraud, corruption, and commercial disputes increases, the demand for forensic accounting expertise has grown. Forensic accountants contribute significantly to the judicial process by providing objective financial analysis, expert opinions, and reliable evidence that enhance the quality and effectiveness of legal decision-making.

The chapter highlighted the dual role of forensic accountants both within and outside the courtroom. Within the courts, their involvement as expert witnesses and expert consultants supports judges and legal practitioners by clarifying complex financial matters, assessing damages, and evaluating opposing expert opinions. Outside the courts, forensic accountants play a pivotal role in alternative dispute resolution mechanisms, including negotiation, mediation, and arbitration, where their financial expertise facilitates informed settlements, reduces litigation costs, and promotes timely dispute resolution [9, 13, 32–36].

Table 5.2 Ethics, skills, and knowledge required for forensic accountants in litigation support

Ethics, skills, and knowledge	Explanation and relation to the forensic accounting role in litigation support
Professional ethics & integrity	Forensic accountants must act with honesty, independence, and objectivity. Ethical conduct ensures the credibility of findings, which is crucial when evidence is presented in court
Confidentiality	Handling sensitive financial and legal information requires strict confidentiality to protect clients and maintain the integrity of legal proceedings
Professional skepticism	The ability to question information and remain alert to potential misstatements or fraud strengthens the reliability of litigation support analysis
Analytical and critical thinking skills	These skills enable forensic accountants to examine complex financial data, identify inconsistencies, and draw defensible conclusions for legal disputes
Investigative skills	Essential for detecting fraud, tracing assets, and reconstructing financial transactions that may be disputed during litigation
Communication skills	Clear written reports and oral testimony are vital, as forensic accountants must explain complex financial issues in a way judges and lawyers can understand
Legal knowledge	Understanding legal procedures, rules of evidence, and litigation processes allows forensic accountants to align their work with court requirements
Accounting and auditing knowledge	A strong grounding in accounting standards and auditing principles helps identify irregularities and accurately assess financial damages
Knowledge of fraud and financial crimes	Awareness of fraud schemes and financial crime techniques enhances the accountant's effectiveness in uncovering wrongdoing in litigation cases
Expert witness skills	The ability to provide unbiased expert opinions and withstand cross-examination supports the forensic accountant's role as a credible witness in court

In addition, the chapter discussed a range of other litigation support services, including compliance program design, matrimonial dispute analysis, and shadow expert engagements, thereby demonstrating the breadth and versatility of forensic accounting practice. The qualifications required to serve effectively as an expert witness were also explored, emphasising that a combination of education, experience, professional credentials, and practical expertise is essential for admissibility and credibility in legal proceedings [33, 37, 38].

Finally, the chapter underscored the importance of ethical conduct, specialised skills, and interdisciplinary knowledge for forensic accountants engaged in litigation support. Professional ethics, analytical and investigative capabilities, legal and accounting knowledge, and effective communication skills are fundamental to ensuring objectivity, reliability, and trustworthiness. Collectively, these competencies position forensic accountants as indispensable contributors to justice, accountability, and the fair resolution of financial disputes [6, 39–43]. As legal and economic systems continue to evolve, the role of forensic accounting in litigation support is expected to expand further, reinforcing its significance as a vital profession at the intersection of accounting and law.

References

1. Taha, R., N. Taha, and H. Ananzeh, *Determinants of litigation risk in the Jordanian financial sector: the role of firm-specific indicators*. Journal of Financial Reporting and Accounting, 2023.
2. Imjai, N., et al., *Empowering generation z accountants in the era of data complexity and open innovation: Nurturing big data analytics, diagnostic, and forensic accounting skills*. Journal of Open Innovation: Technology, Market, and Complexity, 2024: p. 100308.
3. Pham, Q.H. and K.P. Vu, *Insight into how digital forensic accounting and metaverse circular business model innovation contribute to accelerated internationalization: evidence from Vietnam-based SMEs*. Cogent Business & Management, 2024. **11**(1): p. 2320203.
4. Kaur, B., K. Sood, and S. Grima, *A systematic review on forensic accounting and its contribution towards fraud detection and prevention*. Journal of Financial Regulation and Compliance, 2023. **31**(1): p. 60–95.
5. Street, D. and J. Wilck, *'Let's Have a Chat': Principles for the Effective Application of ChatGPT and Large Language Models in the Practice of Forensic Accounting*. Journal of Forensic and Investigative Accounting, July to December, 2023.
6. Alzahrane, M.A., *Insights from forensic accounting educators and practitioners within the KSA context regarding the optimal forensic accounting skills set: an implication on the socio-economic development*. Journal of Business and Socio-economic Development, 2024. **4**(1): p. 66–80.
7. Burnett, J., et al., *A collaboration between adult protective services and forensic accounting examiners to investigate complex financial exploitation: formative evaluation findings*. Journal of Elder Abuse & Neglect, 2024: p. 1–18.
8. Abdul-Baki, Z., *The role of accounting in conflicts resolution: The case of PwC's forensic audit of the Nigerian National Petroleum Corporation*. Managerial Auditing Journal, 2019. **36** (2): p. 261–279.
9. Alshurafat, H., et al., *Forensic accounting core and interdisciplinary curricula components in Australian universities: Analysis of websites*. Journal of Forensic and Investigative Accounting, 2019. **11**(2): p. 353–365.
10. Al Shbeil, S., et al. *What Do We Know About Forensic Accounting? A Literature Review*. in *European, Asian, Middle Eastern, North African Conference on Management & Information Systems*. 2023. Springer.
11. Alkhalaileh, R., et al., *The Impact of External Auditors with Forensic Accounting Competencies on Auditee Firm Performance*. Heliyon, 2024.
12. Alshurafat, H., et al., *Obstacles Facing the Development of Forensic Accounting Curricula within Australian Universities: Exploring Perspectives of Practitioners and Educators*. Australasian Accounting, Business and Finance Journal, 2024. **18**(2): p. 188–195.
13. Alshurafat, H., et al. *The Domain of Forensic Accounting Services: Evidence from Australia*. in *19th Asian Academic Accounting Association (FourA) Annual Conference*. 2019.
14. Crain, M.A., et al., *Essentials of forensic accounting*. 2019: John Wiley & Sons.
15. Al-Hazaima, H., O. Arabiat, and G. Maayah, *The double-edged sword of forensic accounting services: litigation risks in Jordan's industrial sector*. Journal of Financial Reporting and Accounting, 2023.
16. Alkhalaileh, R.I., H. Alshurafat, and H. Al-Hazaima, *Divergence and convergence of salient stakeholders' perceptions toward forensic accounting education: importance, obstacles, and pedagogies*. Journal of Business and Socio-economic Development, 2023.

17. Almashaqbeh, R.N., H. Alshurafat, and H. Al Amosh, *The Impact of Professionalism Theory Constructs on the Applicability of Forensic Accounting Services: Evidence from Jordan.* International Journal of Financial Studies, 2023. **11**(4): p. 141.
18. Cooper, J.R. and B.S. Kawada, *Balboa security v. M&M systems: Forensic accounting for determining commercial damages.* Journal of Accounting Education, 2022. **58**: p. 100755.
19. Alshurafat, H., H.A. Haloush, and A.B.M. Alzoubi, *Forensic accounting from an Islamic perspective: a conceptual framework from the Jordanian context*, in *Islamic Accounting and Finance: A Handbook.* 2023, World Scientific. p. 173–193.
20. Alzoubi, A.B., *Maximizing internal control effectiveness: the synergy between forensic accounting and corporate governance.* Journal of Financial Reporting and Accounting, 2023.
21. Ebaid, I.E.-S., *An exploration of accounting students' attitudes toward integrating forensic accounting in accounting education.* International Journal of Law and Management, 2022(ahead-of-print).
22. Huber, W., et al., *Factors which may bias judges' decisions to exclude accounting expert witnesses testimony.* Accounting Research Journal, 2015. **28**(1): p. 59–77.
23. Honigsberg, C., *Forensic accounting.* Annual Review of Law and Social Science, 2020. **16**: p. 147–164.
24. Durtschi, C. and R.J. Rufus, *Arson or accident: A forensic accounting case requiring critical thinking and expert communication.* Issues in Accounting Education Teaching Notes, 2017. **32**(1): p. 89–105.
25. Huber, W., *Is forensic accounting in the United States becoming a profession?* Journal of Forensic & Investigative Accounting, 2012. **4**(1).
26. Huber, W., *Is forensic accounting in the United States becoming a profession?* Journal of Forensic & Investigative Accounting, 2012. **4**(1): p. 255–284.
27. Howieson, B., et al., *Who should teach what? Australian perceptions of the roles of universities and practice in the education of professional accountants.* Journal of Accounting Education, 2014. **32**(3): p. 259–275.
28. Tarr, J.-A., J. Van Akkeren, and S. Buckby, *Forensic accounting: Professional regulation of a multi-disciplinary field.* Australian Business Law Review, 2016. **44**(3): p. 204–215.
29. Alshurafat, H., *Forensic accounting as a profession in Australia? A sociological perspective.* Meditari Accountancy Research, 2021.
30. Ismail, S., et al., *A Review on Forensic Accounting Profession and Education: Global Context.* 2022.
31. Davis, C., R. Farrell, and S. Ogilby, *Characteristics and skills of the Forensic Accountant.* American Institute of Certified Public Accountants, 2010: p. 11–26.
32. Rezaee, Z., G.H. Lander, and T.A. Gavin, *Forensic accounting in the Curriculum.* Managerial Auditing Journal, 1992.
33. Curtis, G.E., *Legal and regulatory environments and ethics: Essential components of a fraud and forensic accounting curriculum.* Issues in Accounting Education, 2008. **23**(4): p. 535.
34. Alshurafat, H.A., *Forensic accounting curricula and pedagogies in Australian universities: analysis of academic and practitioner perspectives.* 2019, University of Southern Queensland.
35. Alhusban, A.A.A., et al., *The regulatory structure and governance of forensic accountancy in the emerging market: challenges and opportunities.* Journal of Governance and Regulation/ Volume, 2020. **9**(4): p. 149–161.
36. Alshurafat, H., et al., *Perceptions of the usefulness of various teaching methods in forensic accounting education.* Accounting Education, 2020. **29**(2): p. 177–204.
37. Haloush, H.A., H. Alshurafat, and A.A.A. Alhusban, *Auditors'civil liability towards clients under the jordanian law: legal and auditing perspectives.* Journal of Governance and Regulation/Volume, 2021. **10**(1).
38. Mertens, F., *The Use of Artificial Intelligence in Corporate Decision-Making at Board Level: A Preliminary Legal Analysis.* 2023.
39. Carnes, K.C. and N.J. Gierlasinski, *Forensic accounting skills: will supply finally catch up to demand?* Managerial Auditing Journal, 2001. **16**(6): p. 378–382.

40. DiGabriele, J.A., *An empirical investigation of the relevant skills of forensic accountants.* Journal of Education for Business, 2008. **83**(6): p. 331–338.
41. Gbegi, D. and J. Adebisi, *Forensic accounting skills and techniques in fraud investigation in the Nigerian public sector.* Mediterranean Journal of Social Sciences, 2014. **5**(3): p. 243–243.
42. Salleh, K. and R. Ab Aziz, *Traits, skills and ethical values of public sector forensic accountants: an empirical investigation.* Procedia-Social and Behavioral Sciences, 2014. **145**: p. 361–370.
43. Al Natour, A.R., et al., *The role of forensic accounting skills in fraud detection and the moderating effect of CAATTs application: evidence from Egypt.* Journal of Financial Reporting and Accounting, 2023.

Chapter 6
The Role of Forensic Accounting in Business Valuation Services

6.1 Introduction

The field of forensic accounting offers a broad spectrum of services [1, 2]. A key area within this is business valuation, which includes numerous sub-services [3, 4]. In this domain, forensic accountants might assess a company's asset values, evaluate damages arising from insurance claims and contracts, and determine employee compensation, among other services [5, 6].

Forensic accounting employs rigorous investigative methods to support business valuation, particularly in litigation, fraud detection, and dispute resolution, ensuring that valuations reflect the true economic reality amid potential manipulation [3, 5–7]. This chapter systematically outlines 16 core services where forensic accountants excel, from employee incentive verification and hidden asset tracing to intellectual property assessments and merger due diligence, each illustrated with practical examples drawn from real-world disputes. Academic literature underscores their unique ability to reconstruct financial records, quantify damages, and provide expert testimony, thereby bridging the gap between economic analysis and legal proceedings [8–13].

Forensic accountants apply three primary valuation approaches, including income, market, and asset methods, to deliver defensible estimates in forensic contexts.

- The income approach discounts projected cash flows, adjusting for litigation risks like fraud or business interruptions.
- Market methods use comparable transactions and multiples (e.g., P/E, EV/EBITDA) tailored to industry benchmarks, critical for minority interests and M&A.
- Asset-based valuations appraise tangibles and intangibles, essential for insolvency and bankruptcy reconstructions.

H. Alshurafat, *Forensic Accounting*, https://doi.org/10.1007/978-981-95-8613-4_6

These techniques integrate forensic scrutiny, such as liability deep dives and anomaly detection, thereby enhancing accuracy relative to standard appraisals.

In matrimonial and personal injury cases, forensic experts calculate the present value of pensions, lost earnings, and concealed income using bank records and lifestyle analysis.

- Insolvency reveals preferential transfers, supporting creditor recoveries.
- Due diligence uncovers revenue inflation and off-balance-sheet liabilities, protecting buyers.
- Business interruption and contract breach claims rely on hypothetical profit modeling, often yielding insurance payouts or settlements.

Literature highlights forensic accountants' advisory role in minority shareholder oppression, IP infringement losses, and SWOT-informed strategies, where conservative estimates align with judicial preferences [14–18]. Empirical studies affirm the impact on valuation premiums and fraud prevention, positioning forensic accountants as vital in financial forensics [19–26].

6.2 Business Valuation Services

The following subsections outline the services a forensic accountant can provide in business valuation. Additionally, these subsections illustrate the role of forensic accountants in each service and include a real-world example of this role.

6.2.1 Long-Term Employee Incentive

Definition:Long-term incentives reward employees over several years, often through share options or performance bonuses.

Role of Forensic Accountants:They verify incentive calculations and investigate manipulation.

Real-World Example:A senior executive claims that their share options were not paid out after termination. A forensic accountant reviews performance metrics, share valuations, and board approvals to determine the correct entitlement.

6.2.2 Death and Personal Injury

Definition:Claims arising from injury or death due to negligence.

Role of Forensic Accountants:They calculate financial loss and future earnings.

Real-World Example:Following a fatal workplace accident, a forensic accountant calculates lost lifetime earnings and financial dependency for the deceased's family.

6.2.3 *Matrimonial Issues and Hidden Asset Investigations*

Definition:Financial disputes during divorce, including asset division.

Role of Forensic Accountants:They trace concealed income and assets.

Real-World Example:A business owner understates income during divorce proceedings. A forensic accountant analyses bank deposits and company expenses to uncover hidden income streams.

6.2.4 *Superannuation Interests*

Definition:Retirement benefits accumulated during employment.

Role of Forensic Accountants:They value and divide superannuation fairly.

Real-World Example:During a divorce, a forensic accountant calculates the present value of a spouse's defined-benefit pension for court-ordered asset splitting.

6.2.5 *Insolvency and Bankruptcy*

Definition:Inability to meet financial obligations.

Role of Forensic Accountants:They investigate fraud and asset transfers.

Real-World Example:Before declaring bankruptcy, a director transfers assets to relatives. A forensic accountant traces these transfers and reports them to the liquidator.

6.2.6 *Loss and Damage Claims*

Definition:Claims for financial losses caused by wrongdoing.

Role of Forensic Accountants:They quantify actual financial damage.

Real-World Example:A supplier delivers defective machinery, causing production delays. A forensic accountant calculates the business's financial loss for legal action.

6.2.7 Calculating Profits Lost

Definition:Estimating the profits a business would have earned without disruption.

Role of Forensic Accountants:They calculate hypothetical profits.

Real-World Example:A café forced to close for 3 months due to council negligence hires a forensic accountant to calculate profits lost during closure.

6.2.8 Business Interruption

Definition:Disruption of business operations due to insured events.

Role of Forensic Accountants:They assess business interruption insurance claims.

Real-World Example:After a warehouse fire, a forensic accountant calculates lost revenue and ongoing expenses to support an insurance claim.

6.2.9 Breaches of Contract Loss

Definition:Losses arising from failure to honor contractual obligations.

Role of Forensic Accountants:They assess financial damages.

Real-World Example:A contractor abandons a project mid-way. A forensic accountant calculates additional costs incurred to complete the project.

6.2.10 Minority Interests

Definition:Ownership stakes without controlling power.

Role of Forensic Accountants:They value minority shares and assess oppression claims.

Real-World Example:Minority shareholders allege that the majority owners are diverting profits. A forensic accountant investigates financial statements and values the minority stake for a buy-out.

6.2.11 Insurance Claims

Definition:Requests for compensation under insurance policies.

Role of Forensic Accountants:They validate and quantify claims.

Real-World Example:A retail store claims inventory loss after flooding. A forensic accountant verifies stock records and calculates the insurer's actual losses.

6.2.12 *Intellectual Property*

Definition:Intangible assets like patents and trademarks.

Role of Forensic Accountants:They value IP and quantify the losses from infringement.

Real-World Example:A software company sues a competitor for copyright infringement. A forensic accountant calculates lost licensing revenue.

6.2.13 *SWOT Analysis*

Definition:Analysis of strengths, weaknesses, opportunities, and threats.

Role of Forensic Accountants:They support strategic and financial evaluation.

Real-World Example:During a fraud investigation, a forensic accountant uses SWOT analysis to assess the financial vulnerabilities that management exploited.

6.2.14 *Merger and Acquisition*

Definition:Business consolidation through mergers or acquisitions.

Role of Forensic Accountants:They conduct due diligence and risk assessments.

Real-World Example:Before acquiring a company, forensic accountants uncover undisclosed liabilities and inflated revenue figures.

6.2.15 *Reconstruction Records*

Definition:Recreating incomplete or destroyed financial records.

Role of Forensic Accountants:They rebuild accounts using alternative evidence.

Real-World Example:After a flood destroys accounting records, a forensic accountant reconstructs financial statements using bank records and supplier invoices.

6.2.16 *Deliver Estimation of Value*

Definition:Determining the monetary value of an asset or business.

Role of Forensic Accountants:They provide defensible valuations.

Real-World Example:In a shareholder dispute, a forensic accountant values a privately owned company to determine a fair exit price.

6.3 Conclusion

In conclusion, this chapter illustrates the role of forensic accountants in business valuation, transforming complex financial puzzles into clear, defensible insights that underpin justice in litigation, negotiations, and corporate decisions. From verifying long-term employee incentives and tracing hidden assets in matrimonial disputes to reconstructing records after disasters and quantifying intellectual property losses, these professionals blend investigative rigor with valuation expertise, ensuring outcomes that withstand judicial and economic scrutiny. The forensic accountants' work not only resolves immediate conflicts such as insolvency fraud probes or minority shareholder oppression claims but also strengthens broader financial ecosystems by deterring manipulation and promoting transparency in high-stakes environments like mergers, insurance claims, and contract breaches [21, 27–31].

The chapter's exploration of core valuation approaches and real-world examples, from calculating lost profits in business interruptions to delivering SWOT analyses during fraud investigations, reveals how these methods adapt to scenarios, yielding precise damage quantifications that influence settlements, court rulings, and policy reforms [20, 32–36]. Empirical studies affirm that such precision elevates forensic accounting beyond routine audits, adding measurable value through fraud detection and risk mitigation [19, 32, 37–41].

Forensic accountants have emerged as strategic advisors in an era of escalating financial disputes [42–46]. Forensic accountants' proficiency in areas like personal injury loss calculations, superannuation divisions, and due diligence safeguards stakeholders, from grieving families to institutional investors, by delivering unbiased, court-admissible reports grounded in exhaustive evidence trails [47–52]. As businesses face increasing complexity from digital fraud, regulatory shifts, and economic volatility, this expertise is pivotal in preventing crises and maximizing recoveries, underscoring the profession's evolution from reactive sleuths to proactive financial architects.

By cataloging 16 diverse services with practical illustrations, this chapter establishes business valuation as a cornerstone of forensic practice, bridging accounting principles with legal advocacy. It challenges practitioners to uphold ethical standards amid adversarial pressures, while equipping future experts with frameworks for innovative applications, such as AI-enhanced anomaly detection or blockchain-traced asset flows. Ultimately, forensic accountants in valuation do more than assign numbers; they restore equity and foster trust in financial markets, positioning their discipline as a base of modern commerce and justice [1, 2, 4, 6, 14–17, 23–26].

References

1. Burnett, J., et al., *A collaboration between adult protective services and forensic accounting examiners to investigate complex financial exploitation: formative evaluation findings*. Journal of Elder Abuse & Neglect, 2024: p. 1–18.

2. Guellim, N., et al., *Evaluating the perceived value of forensic accounting: a systematic review method.* Discover Sustainability, 2024. **5**(1): p. 351.
3. DiGabriele, J.A. and P.L. Lohrey, *The valuation of economic damages: A case study for the forensic accountant.* Journal of Forensic & Investigative Accounting, 2016. **8**(2): p. 338–348.
4. Alkababji, M.W., et al., *Forensic Accounting Practices: Evaluating the Current Research*, in *Achieving Sustainable Business Through AI, Technology Education and Computer Science: Volume 3: Business Sustainability and Artificial Intelligence Applications.* 2024, Springer. p. 767–777.
5. Yang, C.-H. and K.-C. Lee, *Developing a strategy map for forensic accounting with fraud risk management: An integrated balanced scorecard-based decision model.* Evaluation and program planning, 2020. **80**: p. 101780.
6. Chitimira, H. and S. Munedzi, *An evaluation of customer due diligence and related anti-money laundering measures in the United Kingdom.* Journal of Money Laundering Control, 2023. **26**(7): p. 127–137.
7. Jalilvand, A. and J.W. Kostolansky, *Le Beau Footwear: A business valuation case for a privately held firm.* Issues in Accounting Education, 2016. **31**(4): p. 439–447.
8. Gallagher, H.A., *Vaughn Elementary's innovative teacher evaluation system: Are teacher evaluation scores related to growth in student achievement?* Peabody Journal of Education, 2004. **79**(4): p. 79–107.
9. DiGabriele, J.A., *Combining elements of the fraud triangle and professional skepticism in the valuation of lost profits.* 2009.
10. Huber, D., *Forensic accounting corporations' codes of ethics and standards of practice–a comparison.* International Journal of Accounting, Auditing and Performance Evaluation, 2013. **9**(2): p. 126–152.
11. Durtschi, C. and R.J. Rufus, *Arson or accident: A forensic accounting case requiring critical thinking and expert communication.* Issues in Accounting Education Teaching Notes, 2017. **32**(1): p. 89–105.
12. Elder, R.J. and A.A. Yebba, *The Roslyn school district fraud: Improving school district internal control and financial oversight.* Issues in Accounting Education, 2017. **32**(4): p. 25–39.
13. Grubb, F., *Colonial Virginia's paper money regime, 1755–74: A forensic accounting reconstruction of the data.* Historical Methods: A Journal of Quantitative and Interdisciplinary History, 2017. **50**(2): p. 96–112.
14. Street, D. and J. Wilck, *'Let's Have a Chat': Principles for the Effective Application of ChatGPT and Large Language Models in the Practice of Forensic Accounting.* Journal of Forensic and Investigative Accounting, July to December, 2023.
15. Alshurafat, H., et al., *Obstacles Facing the Development of Forensic Accounting Curricula within Australian Universities: Exploring Perspectives of Practitioners and Educators.* Australasian Accounting, Business and Finance Journal, 2024. **18**(2): p. 188–195.
16. Pham, Q.H. and K.P. Vu, *Insight into how digital forensic accounting and metaverse circular business model innovation contribute to accelerated internationalization: evidence from Vietnam-based SMEs.* Cogent Business & Management, 2024. **11**(1): p. 2320203.
17. Al-Raggad, M., et al., *Unveiling financial crimes: advancing forensic accounting practices and ethical integrity through bibliometric insights.* Safer Communities, 2025. **24**(3): p. 244–264.
18. Işik, B.K., *ETHICS IN FORENSIC ACCOUNTING: CHALLENGES, IMPACTS AND FUTURE DIRECTIONS.* Anadolu Üniversitesi İktisadi ve İdari Bilimler Fakültesi Dergisi, 2025. **26**(3): p. 316–337.
19. Davidyan, J., et al., *Two Truths and a Lie: Introduction to Deception Detection.* Issues in Accounting Education, 2022.
20. Al Natour, A.R., et al., *The role of forensic accounting skills in fraud detection and the moderating effect of CAATTs application: evidence from Egypt.* Journal of Financial Reporting and Accounting, 2023.

21. Al-Hazaima, H., O. Arabiat, and G. Maayah, *The double-edged sword of forensic accounting services: litigation risks in Jordan's industrial sector.* Journal of Financial Reporting and Accounting, 2023.
22. Alkhalaileh, R.I., H. Alshurafat, and H. Al-Hazaima, *Divergence and convergence of salient stakeholders' perceptions toward forensic accounting education: importance, obstacles and pedagogies.* Journal of Business and Socio-economic Development, 2023.
23. Alshurafat, H., et al. *Forensic Accounting Education Within the Australian Universities.* in *International Conference on Business and Technology*. 2023. Springer.
24. Alzoubi, A.B., *Maximizing internal control effectiveness: the synergy between forensic accounting and corporate governance.* Journal of Financial Reporting and Accounting, 2023.
25. Clavería Navarrete, A. and A. Carrasco Gallego, *Forensic accounting tools for fraud deterrence: a qualitative approach.* Journal of Financial Crime, 2023. **30**(3): p. 840–854.
26. Kaur, B., K. Sood, and S. Grima, *A systematic review on forensic accounting and its contribution towards fraud detection and prevention.* Journal of Financial Regulation and Compliance, 2023. **31**(1): p. 60–95.
27. Utama, A. and B. Basuki, *Exploration of themes based twitter data in fraud-forensic accounting studies.* Cogent Business & Management, 2022. **9**(1): p. 2135207.
28. Yusuf, M. and K. Harefa. *Forensic Accounting and Compliance Audit to Reduce the Number of Financial Fraud in Local Government.* in *2nd International Conference of Strategic Issues on Economics, Business and, Education (ICoSIEBE 2021)*. 2022. Atlantis Press.
29. Afriyie, S.O., et al., *Forensic accounting: A novel paradigm and relevant knowledge in fraud detection and prevention.* International Journal of Public Administration, 2023. **46**(9): p. 615–624.
30. Akinbowale, O.E., H.E. Klingelhöfer, and M.F. Zerihun, *Application of forensic accounting techniques in the South African banking industry for the purpose of fraud risk mitigation.* Cogent Economics & Finance, 2023. **11**(1): p. 2153412.
31. Al Shbeil, S., et al. *What Do We Know About Forensic Accounting? A Literature Review.* in *European, Asian, Middle Eastern, North African Conference on Management & Information Systems*. 2023. Springer.
32. Ebaid, I.E.-S., *An exploration of accounting students' attitudes toward integrating forensic accounting in accounting education.* International Journal of Law and Management, 2022(ahead-of-print).
33. Ismail, S., et al., *A Review on Forensic Accounting Profession and Education: Global Context.* 2022.
34. Mehta, K., et al. *Analyzing the Impact of Forensic Accounting in the Detection of Financial Fraud: The Mediating Role of Artificial Intelligence.* in *International Conference on Innovative Computing and Communications*. 2022. Springer.
35. Nasrallah, N.H., R. El Khoury, and E. Harb, *Forensic Accounting in a Digital Environment: A New Proposed Model*, in *Handbook of Research on the Significance of Forensic Accounting Techniques in Corporate Governance*. 2022, IGI Global. p. 128–149.
36. Rezaee, Z. and J. Wang, *Integration of Big Data into Forensic Accounting Education and Practice: A Survey of Academics in China and the United States.* Journal of Forensic and Investigative Accounting, 2022. **14**(1).
37. Wahyuni-TD, I.S., H. Haron, and Y. Fernando, *The effects of good governance and fraud prevention on performance of the zakat institutions in Indonesia: a Sharīʿah forensic accounting perspective.* International Journal of Islamic and Middle Eastern Finance and Management, 2021. **14**(4): p. 692–712.
38. Afriyie, S.O., et al., *Forensic accounting: a novel paradigm and relevant knowledge in fraud detection and prevention.* International Journal of Public Administration, 2022: p. 1–10.
39. Burzinji, Z., et al., *The effect of forensic accounting on fraud prevention, the moderating role internal control effectiveness.* International Journal of Economics, Commerce and Management, 2022. **10**(1): p. 213–230.

40. Clavería Navarrete, A. and A. Carrasco Gallego, *Forensic accounting tools for fraud deterrence: a qualitative approach.* Journal of Financial Crime, 2022.
41. Cooper, J.R. and B.S. Kawada, *Balboa security v. M&M systems: Forensic accounting for determining commercial damages.* Journal of Accounting Education, 2022. **58**: p. 100755.
42. Alshurafat, H., M.O. Al Shbail, and E. Mansour, *Strengths and weaknesses of forensic accounting: an implication on the socio-economic development.* Journal of Business and Socio-economic Development, 2021.
43. Ghofur, R.A. and A. Santika. *The Influence of Sharia Complaince Against Fraud on The Sharia Banks in Indonesia.* in *Annual Conference of Ihtifaz: Islamic Economics, Finance, and Banking*. 2021.
44. Odia, J.O. and O.T. Akpata, *Role of Data Science and Data Analytics in Forensic Accounting and Fraud Detection*, in *Handbook of Research on Engineering, Business, and Healthcare Applications of Data Science and Analytics*. 2021, IGI Global. p. 203–227.
45. Prabowo, H.Y., *Undergraduate Forensic Accounting Education in Indonesia: Initiating a Re-Invention.* Australasian Accounting, Business and Finance Journal, 2021. **15**(2): p. 3–25.
46. Van Akkeren, J.K. and J.-A. Tarr, *The application of experiential learning for forensic accounting students: the Mock trial.* Accounting Education, 2021: p. 1–28.
47. Sahdan, M.H., C.J. Cowton, and J.E. Drake, *Forensic accounting services in English local government and the counter-fraud agenda.* Public Money & Management, 2020. **40**(5): p. 380–389.
48. Akinbowale, O.E., H.E. Klingelhöfer, and M.F. Zerihun, *The integration of forensic accounting and the management control system as tools for combating cyberfraud.* Academy of Accounting and Financial Studies Journal, 2021. **25**(2): p. 1–14.
49. Al Shbail, M.O., et al., *Dataset of Factors affecting online cheating by accounting students: The relevance of social factors and the fraud triangle model factors.* Data in Brief, 2021: p. 107732.
50. Al Shbail, M.O., et al., *Factors affecting online cheating by accounting students: the relevance of social factors and the fraud triangle model factors.* Academy of Strategic Management Journal, 2021. **20**: p. 1–16.
51. Alshurafat, H., *Forensic accounting as a profession in Australia? A sociological perspective.* Meditari Accountancy Research, 2021.
52. Alshurafat, H., M. Al Shbail, and M. Almuiet, *Factors Affecting the Intention to Adopt IT Forensic Accounting Tools to Detect Financial Cybercrimes.* International Journal of Business Excellence, 2021.

Chapter 7
The Role of Forensic Accounting in Detecting and Preventing Digital and Online Crimes

7.1 Introduction

Digital forensics is the process of collecting and preserving evidence from computers and networks [1]. It helps identify who committed the digital and online crime, recover lost files or emails, repair corrupted data, and determine what happened [2]. There are different types of investigation in the digital environment, such as computer and network forensics, and some investigators focus on devices like phones or specific computer systems [3]. Digital forensics is continually evolving as new technologies emerge, including smartphones and other smart devices [4–7]. This chapter illustrates the role of forensic accounting in detecting and preventing digital and online crimes.

Forensic accountants need to understand digital forensics to investigate financial crimes [8–10]. They must collect and organize evidence to be prepared for court [11, 12]. Typically, a lawyer retains a forensic accountant to maintain the case's confidentiality [13]. The accountant gathers electronic evidence, sometimes with expert assistance, and ensures that all evidence is handled properly [5, 14, 15].

Computer and digital forensics closely parallel traditional crime scene forensics [3]. Just as investigators collect and preserve physical evidence such as fingerprints or DNA, computer forensic specialists gather and preserve digital evidence to ensure it remains reliable and admissible in court [16, 17]. Moreover, key responsibilities for the forensic accountants in the digital crime area include protecting evidence from alteration, determining what evidence to collect, properly storing and cataloging it, maintaining a documented chain of custody, and collaborating with on-site investigators [18–20].

H. Alshurafat, *Forensic Accounting*, https://doi.org/10.1007/978-981-95-8613-4_7

7.2 The Nature of Forensic Accountant Work in the Digital Environment

Computer forensics is similar to the work of traditional forensic scientists and crime scene investigators (CSIs), who examine evidence such as fingerprints, DNA, and trace evidence. Investigations usually begin with crime scene processing, during which a CSI arrives and collects evidence related to the case [21].

To collect and preserve evidence effectively, investigators need to address several important factors. They must prevent the crime scene and evidence from being altered, since compromised evidence could be questioned or dismissed in court [22, 23]. Investigators also decide which evidence to gather based on the suspected crime [7, 13, 14, 18, 20]. Police departments often have specialized divisions, such as homicide, burglary, economic crime, or special victims units, with investigators trained in particular evidence types. General forensic units, such as fingerprint departments, may also support several investigation teams [24–26].

Evidence is gathered systematically. Physical items are stored in secure containers, carefully labeled, and cataloged, with photographs often taken to document the scene [3]. Maintaining a safe, well-documented chain of custody from the time evidence is collected is just as crucial. Any break in this process can weaken the reliability or admissibility of the evidence. Investigators also collaborate closely with detectives or forensic investigators, following their guidance but also providing recommendations based on their expertise and observations [27–30]. After evidence is collected, it is sent to a forensic lab for further examination. IT forensic scientists analyze and interpret evidence. Once their analysis is complete, they write a forensic report outlining the case's main findings [3].

7.3 Skills and Knowledge for a Forensic Accountant in IT Forensics

Sometimes, a computer forensic specialist may transport a computer to the lab, just as an investigator would collect a weapon from a crime scene. In other cases, it might be necessary to copy data from networked systems, much as it is to gather biological samples from a physical scene. Therefore, a forensic accountant needs skills in handling digital evidence, including gathering, transporting, and collecting it [31, 32]. If they have enough technical knowledge, the forensic accountants can extract data directly from computer networks [24, 33]. However, taking computers can disrupt business operations, so this is done only if crucial data needs to be secured immediately to prevent loss or destruction.

Forensic accountants may also work with a client's employees, including IT staff, to help retrieve digital evidence, as long as those people are not suspected of any wrongdoing. Therefore, a forensic accountant must possess communication skills [34–36]. Forensic accountants should assume all gathered evidence may be scrutinized in court. Consequently, they need a basic understanding of the legal issues surrounding digital evidence [37–39].

Unlike physical searches, digital storage devices can hold vast, diverse data in a small space. Investigators may find unrelated evidence, raising legal questions about admissibility. Defining a digital search or seizure is challenging. For example, scrolling through a document may or may not constitute a new search, and copying data may or may not constitute a new search.

7.4 Computer Forensics Responsibilities

In large law enforcement agencies, work is often divided among specialized roles to improve efficiency and effectiveness. The following are forensic accounting roles in detecting and investigating fraud in the digital environment [3].

- Large law enforcement agencies divide work among specialized roles for efficiency and effectiveness.
- Computer forensic technicians/examiners collect digital evidence from computers and networks, either on-site or in a lab.
- Detectives/investigators oversee cases, supervise technicians, communicate with labs, prepare reports, and testify in court.
- Lead investigators must have crime-specific experience.
- Computer forensic scientists organize/analyze digital evidence and prepare legal reports and testimony.
- For financial/economic crimes, forensic accountants or fraud examiners handle investigations.
- Large forensic labs require lab assistants and managers for operational support and workflow management.
- In smaller/simple cases, one skilled investigator may perform all roles (e.g., a forensic accountant handling an embezzlement case independently).

In smaller or less complex investigations, a single skilled investigator may perform all of these roles. For instance, a forensic accountant investigating suspected embezzlement may simply seize the suspect's computer and conduct the analysis independently in their own office.

7.5 Qualifications

Table 7.1 shows the available certifications for forensic accountants in the domain of digital financial crimes.

Table 7.1 Certifications available to a forensic accountant in digital crime investigation

Eligibility	Focus	Certification name	Certifying organization
Limited to certain law enforcement, government employees, and government contractors	Computer forensic examination	Certified Forensic Computer Examiner (CFCE)	International Association of Computer Investigative Specialists (IACIS)
Limited to certain law enforcement, government employees, and government contractors	Advanced Windows forensics	Certified Advanced Windows Forensic Examiner	International Association of Computer Investigative Specialists (IACIS)
Open to individuals meeting training and experience requirements	Basic Level	Certified Computer Crime Investigator	High-Tech Crime Network (HTCN)
Open to individuals meeting training and experience requirements	Advanced Level	Certified Computer Crime Investigator	High-Tech Crime Network (HTCN)
Open to individuals meeting training and experience requirements	Basic Level	Certified Computer Forensic Technician	High-Tech Crime Network (HTCN)
Open to individuals meeting training and experience requirements	Advanced Level	Certified Computer Forensic Technician	High-Tech Crime Network (HTCN)
Open to qualified candidates	Digital forensic examination	AccessData Certified Examiner (ACE)	AccessData
Open to qualified candidates	Mobile device forensics	AccessData Mobile Examiner	AccessData

7.6 Digital Forensics Labs

Collected evidence is sent to forensic labs for analysis and reporting by forensic scientists. In digital investigations, computers or data are seized or copied for forensic analysis [3]. Lab specifications depend on case volume but must meet certain core requirements:

- Secure evidence lockers with tightly controlled keys or programmable locks; large labs have separate storage rooms.
- Secure access systems.
- Secure trash processing.
- Wide range of computers and digital devices, including outdated ones, to process various storage media.
- Ample storage media supplies for making copies of incoming devices.
- Specialized forensic software for different investigative tasks.
- Dedicated workstations for lengthy forensic examinations.
- Disaster-resistant evidence lockers and continuity/disaster recovery plans for emergencies.

- Maintenance of visitor and evidence logs to track all entries, exits, and evidence movements.

The labs assist with many types of crime, especially the following:

- Terrorism
- Crimes of violence
- Trade secret theft
- Theft or destruction of intellectual property
- Financial crime
- Property crime
- Internet crime

7.7 Sub IT Forensic Services

Within the IT forensics domain, a forensic accountant may provide a different set of services [3]. In addition to the set mentioned in Chap. 1, this chapter highlights the following services.

- Data recovery: restoring inaccessible or misplaced files, or data transferred elsewhere.
- On-site acquisition: obtaining information directly from devices that must remain operational.
- Electronic risk control: minimizing threats to electronic information.
- Password recovery: regaining access when passwords are forgotten or deliberately withheld.
- Cell phone forensics: examining phone records and retrieving erased messages.
- Tracing hostile contact: tracking down senders of harassing emails.
- Cyber evidence: recovering digital proof, including deleted information.
- Internet monitoring: observing web usage for policy adherence or criminal behavior.
- Litigation support: offering expert opinions and court testimony on digital matters.

7.8 E-Mail Investigation Cases

E-mail investigations generally fall into two categories: analyzing e-mail as evidence in crimes, abuse, or lawsuits, and identifying the source of specific messages. The first involves searching, retrieving, and examining messages by criteria such as sender, date range, or content, using techniques like content mining and social network analysis to uncover fraud or identify accomplices. The second focuses on tracing message origins through internal headers or document characteristics [40].

7.9 Investigation Tools

The following are the main tools available to a forensic accountant for investigating digital financial crime.

- Documents: forensic accountant searches public and hidden records.
- Questioning: a forensic accountant conducts in-depth interviews to detect deception.
- Confirmations: a forensic accountant also searches for undisclosed accounts.
- Evidence: forensic accountant analyzes physical and electronic evidence in labs.
- Analysis: a forensic accountant examines electronic data for intentional fraud.
- Observation: a forensic accountant uses surveillance techniques.

7.10 Forensics Software Tools

Several computer forensics software tools are available, such as Forensic Toolkit (FTK) and advanced digital forensics and computer-assisted audit (CAATs). This software helps forensic accountants detect digital crimes by uncovering hidden, deleted, or altered data across multiple devices and systems [29]. The following are summary of the software capabilities.

- Password recovery: Brute force and dictionary attacks, including custom dictionaries.
- File recovery: Restore permanently deleted files and data from slack space.
- Hidden data access: Analyze system, cache, page, and registry files.
- Unallocated space analysis: Examine free storage for deleted or hidden files.
- Exact duplication: Create bit-for-bit copies of computers and storage devices.
- Indexing & search: Rapidly search large numbers of files with context-based queries.
- Metadata, logs, and headers analysis: Extract hidden information from files, e-mails, and logs.
- Organization & case management: Catalog images, files, and data systematically for investigations.
- Database and accounting system access: Analyze financial data and monitor controls.
- Activity logging & reporting: Record examiner actions and generate reports for legal use.
- Volatile memory extraction: Acquire data from RAM before it is lost.
- Device versatility: Collect evidence from computers, phones, tablets, and network storage.

7.11 Scenarios for Forensic Accounting Investigation Within the IT Forensic Services

- **Payroll Manipulation Case**
  A forensic accountant discovers that an employee altered payroll system logs to pay themselves overtime for hours never worked.
- **Vendor Overbilling Scheme**
  Digital analysis reveals that a fake vendor was created in the accounting system, with payments routed to a manager's personal account.
- **Insider Trading Alert**
  Email metadata and transaction timestamps show that an executive accessed confidential financial reports shortly before suspicious stock trades.
- **Expense Report Fraud**
  A forensic accountant uncovered edited receipt files and duplicate submissions through metadata analysis.
- **Ghost Employee Scheme**
  System access logs reveal salary payments to employees who no longer exist in the company database.
- **Financial Statement Manipulation**
  A forensic accountant identifies altered spreadsheet formulas used to inflate quarterly revenue figures.
- **Credit Card Abuse**
  Transaction logs show repeated personal purchases charged to a corporate credit card after business hours.
- **Kickback Arrangement**
  Email communications reveal a secret agreement between a purchasing manager and a supplier to inflate contract prices.
- **Data Deletion Cover-Up**
  Deleted accounting records have been recovered, indicating an attempt to hide unauthorized fund transfers.
- **Inventory Fraud**
  System discrepancies between inventory records and physical stock point to falsified digital entries.
- **Unauthorized System Access**
  Login records reveal that a former employee continued accessing financial systems after termination.
- **Tax Evasion Attempt**
  Digital accounting records show deliberate income misclassification to reduce reported tax liabilities.
- **Procurement Card Fraud**
  Analysis of transaction timing and vendor data uncovers misuse of procurement cards for personal expenses.

- **False Refund Scheme**
  A forensic accountant identifies repeated customer refunds issued to accounts linked to an employee.
- **Budget Manipulation**
  Version history in budgeting software reveals unauthorized changes made to shift funds between departments

7.12 Conclusion

Forensic accounting has emerged as a vital discipline in combating digital and online financial crimes. The integration of accounting expertise with digital forensics enables the systematic collection, preservation, and analysis of electronic evidence, which is crucial for legal proceedings and fraud prevention. Forensic accountants must possess a diverse skill set that includes technical knowledge, investigative techniques, legal awareness, and communication abilities to operate effectively in the digital environment. The availability of specialized certifications, software tools, and forensic laboratories further enhances their capability to address complex cybercrime scenarios, from payroll manipulation and insider trading to data deletion and procurement fraud. As digital technologies continue to evolve, the role of forensic accounting will become increasingly central to ensuring financial integrity, protecting organizational assets, and supporting law enforcement efforts. Continuous professional development, interdisciplinary collaboration, and adherence to ethical standards are essential to maintaining the effectiveness and credibility of forensic accounting in the digital age.

References

1. Imjai, N., et al., *Empowering generation Z accountants in the era of data complexity and open innovation: Nurturing big data analytics, diagnostic, and forensic accounting skills*. Journal of Open Innovation: Technology, Market, and Complexity, 2024: p. 100308.
2. Alkababji, M.W., et al., *Forensic Accounting Practices: Evaluating the Current Research*, in *Achieving Sustainable Business Through AI, Technology Education and Computer Science: Volume 3: Business Sustainability and Artificial Intelligence Applications*. 2024, Springer. p. 767–777.
3. Crain, M.A., et al., *Essentials of forensic accounting*. 2019: John Wiley & Sons.
4. Al Shbeil, S., et al. *What Do We Know About Forensic Accounting? A Literature Review*. in *European, Asian, Middle Eastern, North African Conference on Management & Information Systems*. 2023. Springer.
5. Alsadah, N. and A. Al-Sartawi, *Forensic Accounting and Cybersecurity: A Literature Review Paper*. Artificial Intelligence, Internet of Things, and Society 5.0, 2023: p. 235–244.
6. Kaur, B., K. Sood, and S. Grima, *A systematic review on forensic accounting and its contribution towards fraud detection and prevention*. Journal of Financial Regulation and Compliance, 2023. **31**(1): p. 60–95.

7. Ozili, P.K., *Forensic accounting research around the world.* Journal of Financial Reporting and Accounting, 2023.
8. Clavería Navarrete, A. and A. Carrasco Gallego, *Forensic accounting tools for fraud deterrence: a qualitative approach.* Journal of Financial Crime, 2023. **30**(3): p. 840–854.
9. Alzoubi, A.B., *Maximizing internal control effectiveness: the synergy between forensic accounting and corporate governance.* Journal of Financial Reporting and Accounting, 2023.
10. Digabriele, J., *An empirical investigation of the relevant skills of forensic accountants.* Journal of education for business, 2008. **83**(6): p. 331–338.
11. Curtis, G.E., *Legal and regulatory environments and ethics: Essential components of a fraud and forensic accounting curriculum.* Issues in Accounting Education, 2008. **23**(4): p. 535.
12. Curtis, G.E., *The model curriculum in fraud and forensic accounting and economic crime programs at Utica College.* Issues in Accounting Education, 2008. **23**(4): p. 581–592.
13. Alkhalaileh, R., et al., *The impact of external auditors with forensic accounting competencies on auditee firm performance.* Heliyon, 2024. **10**(11).
14. Rezaee, Z. and J. Wang, *Integration of Big Data into Forensic Accounting Education and Practice: A Survey of Academics in China and the United States.* Journal of Forensic and Investigative Accounting, 2022. **14**(1).
15. Alkhalaileh, R.I., H. Alshurafat, and H. Al-Hazaima, *Divergence and convergence of salient stakeholders' perceptions toward forensic accounting education: importance, obstacles, and pedagogies.* Journal of Business and Socio-economic Development, 2023. **4**(2): p. 127–141.
16. Pham, Q.H. and K.P. Vu, *Insight into how digital forensic accounting and metaverse circular business model innovation contribute to accelerated internationalization: evidence from Vietnam-based SMEs.* Cogent Business & Management, 2024. **11**(1): p. 2320203.
17. Al-Raggad, M., et al., *Unveiling financial crimes: advancing forensic accounting practices and ethical integrity through bibliometric insights.* Safer Communities, 2025. **24**(3): p. 244–264.
18. Nasrallah, N.H., R. El Khoury, and E. Harb, *Forensic Accounting in a Digital Environment: A New Proposed Model*, in *Handbook of Research on the Significance of Forensic Accounting Techniques in Corporate Governance*. 2022, IGI Global. p. 128–149.
19. Ahmad, S., M.S. Ibrahim, and R.M. Abdou, *Understanding the Role of Forensic Accountants in Due Diligence Within Organizations and Its Impact on Organizational Learning.* Sustainable Data Management: Navigating Big Data, Communication Technology, and Business Digital Leadership. Volume 1, 2025: p. 3–10.
20. Ismail, S., R.M. Abdou, and M.S. Ibrahim, *Who is Better in Practicing Customer Due Diligence as an Anti-Money Laundering Tool for Financial Institutions: Can Internal Auditors Be Forensic Accountants? Evidence from MENA Region*, in *Sustainable Data Management: Navigating Big Data, Communication Technology, and Business Digital Leadership. Volume 1*. 2025, Springer. p. 11–23.
21. Seda, M.A., B. Peterson Kramer, and D.L. Crumbley, *An examination of computer forensics and related certifications in the accounting curriculum.* Journal of Digital Forensics, Security and Law, 2019. **14**(1): p. 4.
22. Pearson, T.A. and T.W. Singleton, *Fraud and forensic accounting in the digital environment.* Issues in Accounting Education, 2008. **23**(4): p. 545.
23. Saal, M., S. Starnes, and T. Rehermann, *Digital Financial Services.* 2017.
24. Gbegi, D. and J. Adebisi, *Forensic accounting skills and techniques in fraud investigation in the Nigerian public sector.* Mediterranean Journal of Social Sciences, 2014. **5**(3): p. 243–243.
25. Tarr, J.-A., J. Van Akkeren, and S. Buckby, *Forensic accounting: Professional regulation of a multi-disciplinary field.* Australian Business Law Review, 2016. **44**(3): p. 204–215.
26. Wang, J., G. Lee, and D.L. Crumbley, *Current Availability of Forensic Accounting Education and State of Forensic Accounting Services in Hong Kong and Mainland China.* Journal of Forensic and Investigative Accounting, 2016. **8**(3): p. 515–534.
27. Alshurafat, H., et al., *Forensic accounting core and interdisciplinary curricula components in Australian universities: Analysis of websites.* Journal of Forensic and Investigative Accounting, 2019. **11**(2): p. 353–365.

28. Alshurafat, H., et al. *The Domain of Forensic Accounting Services: Evidence from Australia.* in *19th Asian Academic Accounting Association (FourA) Annual Conference.* 2019.
29. Alshurafat, H., M. Al Shbail, and M. Almuiet, *Factors Affecting the Intention to Adopt IT Forensic Accounting Tools to Detect Financial Cybercrimes.* International Journal of Business Excellence, 2021.
30. Alshurafat, H., M.O. Al Shbail, and E. Mansour, *Strengths and weaknesses of forensic accounting: an implication on the socio-economic development.* Journal of Business and Socio-economic Development, 2021.
31. Al Natour, A.R., et al., *The role of forensic accounting skills in fraud detection and the moderating effect of CAATTs application: evidence from Egypt.* Journal of Financial Reporting and Accounting, 2023.
32. Alzahrane, M.A., *Insights from forensic accounting educators and practitioners within the KSA context regarding the optimal forensic accounting skills set: an implication on the socio-economic development.* Journal of Business and Socio-economic Development, 2024. **4**(1): p. 66–80.
33. Salleh, K. and R. Ab Aziz, *Traits, skills and ethical values of public sector forensic accountants: an empirical investigation.* Procedia-Social and Behavioral Sciences, 2014. **145**: p. 361–370.
34. Davis, C., R. Farrell, and S. Ogilby, *Characteristics and skills of the Forensic Accountant*, in *American Institute of Certified Public Accountants.* 2010.
35. McMullen, D.A. and M.H. Sanchez, *A preliminary investigation of the necessary skills, education requirements, and training requirements for forensic accountants.* Journal of Forensic & Investigative Accounting, 2010. **2**(2): p. 30–48.
36. Stone, G., M. Lightbody, and R. Whait, *Developing accounting students' listening skills: Barriers, opportunities and an integrated stakeholder approach.* Accounting Education, 2013. **22**(2): p. 168–192.
37. Carnes, K.C. and N.J. Gierlasinski, *Forensic accounting skills: will supply finally catch up to demand?* Managerial Auditing Journal, 2001. **16**(6): p. 378–382.
38. Davidson, R.A. and B.A. Baldwin, *Cognitive skills objectives in intermediate accounting textbooks: Evidence from end-of-chapter material.* Journal of Accounting Education, 2005. **23**(2): p. 79–95.
39. DiGabriele, J.A., *An empirical investigation of the relevant skills of forensic accountants.* Journal of Education for Business, 2008. **83**(6): p. 331–338.
40. Isacenkova, J., et al., *Inside the scam jungle: A closer look at 419 scam email operations.* EURASIP Journal on Information Security, 2014. **2014**(1): p. 4.

Index

A
Accountability, 9, 11–13, 16–19, 51, 57, 62
Accounting education, 4
Accounting profession, 9
American Institute of Certified Public Accountants (AICPA), 5, 7, 10, 18, 19
Anti-bribery, 3
Anti-corruption, 11–13, 15, 17–19
Anti-Money Laundering & Counter-Terrorist Financing (AML/CFT), 13, 14, 17
Anti-Money Laundering Unit – Jordan (AMLU), 13, 17
Arbitration, 55, 59–61
Asset misappropriation, 4, 27, 29–31, 34
Asset tracing, 13, 67
Auditing *vs.* forensic accounting, 12, 14

B
Banking sector, 14, 17, 44
Bias (ethical and cognitive), 12, 13
Bid rigging, 27
Bribery, 19, 26, 27, 33
Business interruption, 4, 67, 68, 70, 72
Business valuation, 1, 2, 5, 6, 60, 67–72

C
Certified Forensic Accountant (Cr.FA), 5, 7
Certified Fraud Examiner (CFE), 6, 7
Certified Information Systems Auditor (CISA), 6
Chain of custody, 15–17, 77, 78
Confidentiality, 11, 12, 14, 16–19, 60, 62, 77
Conflicts of interest, 9–12, 17–19, 26–28, 31
Corporate governance, 2, 14, 17, 40, 48
Corruption schemes, 26, 27
Court testimony, 81
Cross-examination, 57, 59, 61, 62
Cybercrime, 6, 84

D
Data mining, 3
Data preservation, 3
Data visualization, 3
Digital forensics, 2, 77, 80–82, 84
Dispute resolution, 2, 55, 57–61, 67
Due diligence, 13, 17, 67, 68, 71, 72

E
Economic extortion, 26, 27
E-discovery, 3
Electronic financial crimes, 2, 6
Employee dishonesty, 4
Ethical codes of conducts, 10, 18–19
Ethics (forensic accounting), 19
Expert consulting, 2, 57
Expert witness, 2, 5, 6, 18, 55–57, 59–62

F
Financial crimes, 2, 4, 7, 25, 36, 43–51, 55, 62, 77, 79, 81, 82, 84
Financial statement fraud, 34, 49
Forensic accounting (definition, scope, evolution), 1, 9, 16, 20
Forensic accounting education, 4

H. Alshurafat, *Forensic Accounting*, https://doi.org/10.1007/978-981-95-8613-4

Forensic accounting profession, 1–7, 10, 16, 20
Forensic ethics, 12
Fraud detection, 1, 2, 12, 35, 40, 67, 72
Fraud examination, 2, 12
Fraud investigation, 1, 5, 12, 25–40, 71, 72
Fraud prevention, 6, 7, 35, 68, 84
Fraud tree, 26, 32

G
Government sector, 6
Governance mechanisms, 35

H
Healthcare fraud, 6

I
Identity theft, 33, 43, 48–50
Independence, 11, 12, 16–19, 57, 62
Industrial sector, 6
Insider trading, 14, 17, 83, 84
Insurance claims, 2, 33, 67, 70, 72
Integrity, 9, 11–13, 15–19, 21, 36, 40, 51, 57, 62, 84
Intellectual property theft, 6
International ethical standards, 11, 15
IT forensics, 1, 5, 78–79, 81, 83–84

J
Jordanian Association of Certified Public Accountants (JACPA), 11, 15, 17
Jordanian Companies Law, 13
Jordan Integrity and Anti-Corruption Commission (JIACC), 11–14, 17
Jordan Securities Commission (JSC), 14, 17

L
Litigation support, 1, 2, 5, 7, 55–63, 81
Loss and damage claims, 3, 69

M
Mediation, 57, 58, 60, 61
Minority interests, 67
Money laundering, 6, 13, 43, 44, 46, 47, 49, 50

O
Objectivity, 11, 12, 16–19, 62
Occupational fraud, 25–27, 32, 34, 35

P
Professional behavior, 16–19
Professional certification, 12
Professional competence and due care, 16, 18, 19
Public interest, 16–18

R
Regulatory compliance, 2, 6, 16, 17
Risk assessments, 58, 71

S
Securities fraud, 17, 39
Shadow expert, 62
Skimming, 27, 29
Social responsibility, 12
Standards of evidence, 59
System security, 3

T
Technology in accounting, 6, 13
Transparency, 6, 11, 12, 16–19, 51, 72

V
Valuation analyst, 7
Vendor fraud, 6, 28, 32

W
Whistleblowing, 19